OHIO STAR QUILTS

QUILTS

New Quilts from an Old Favorite

OHIO STAR QUILTS

New Quilts from an Old Favorite

Edited by Victoria Faoro

American Quilter's Society

P.O. Box 3290, Paducah, KY 42002-3290

Dedication

This book is dedicated to quiltmakers
of all times and all places, whose works
continue to inspire and delight.

Ohio star quilts: new quilts from an old favorite / edited by
    Victoria Faoro.
        p.   cm.
    Includes indexes.
    ISBN 0-89145-869-7
    1. Patchwork--Patterns.   2. Quilting--Patterns.   3. Patchwork
quilts.   4. Stars in art.   I. Faoro, Victoria.
    TT835.0395   1996
    746.46'041--dc20   96-15484
                                                                          CIP

Located in Paducah, Kentucky, the American Quilter's Society (AQS) is dedicated to promoting the accomplishments of today's quilters. Through its publications and events, AQS strives to honor today's quiltmakers and their work – and inspire future creativity and innovation in quiltmaking.

Additional copies of this book may be ordered from: American Quilter's Society, P.O. Box 3290, Paducah, KY 42002-3290 @ $16.95. Add $2.00 for postage & handling.

Copyright: 1996, American Quilter's Society

Exhibitions

LOG CABIN QUILTS: NEW QUILTS FROM AN OLD FAVORITE
1995 CONTEST

Museum of the American Quilter's Society, Paducah, Kentucky, March 4 – June 3, 1995
Octagon Center for the Arts, Ames, Iowa, June 11 – August 6, 1995
Topeka & Shawnee Co. Public Museum, Topeka, Kansas, July 12 – August 31, 1996

OHIO STAR QUILTS: NEW QUILTS FROM AN OLD FAVORITE
1996 CONTEST

Museum of the American Quilter's Society, Paducah, Kentucky, January 6 – May 11, 1996
Powers Museum, Carthage, Missouri, October 1 – November 17, 1996
Minnesota Quilt Festival, Duluth, Minnesota, June 2 – 16, 1997
Octagon Center for the Arts, Ames, Iowa, September 2 – November 2, 1997

Please reconfirm dates with the institutions.

For a current exhibition schedule or to schedule a booking, write:
MAQS
P.O. Box 1540
Paducah, KY 42002-1540

Table of Contents

Foreword

This book has been developed in conjunction with an annual Museum of the American Quilter's Society (MAQS) contest and exhibit entitled "New Quilts from Old Favorites." Dedicated to honoring today's quilter, MAQS has created this contest to recognize and share with others the fascinating array of interpretations that can grow out of a single traditional quilt pattern.

A brief introduction to the contest is followed by a presentation of the 18 finalists, including the five winners of awards. Full-color photographs of the quilts are accompanied by their makers' comments, which provide fascinating insights. Full-size templates for the traditional pattern enable anyone to make an Ohio Star quilt, minus the work of having to draft the templates needed. The tips, techniques, and patterns contributed by the winning contestants make a wide range of quilts easier to execute in fabric.

It is our hope that this combination of outstanding quilts, full-size patterns, and instructional information will inspire as many outstanding quilts as the original contest did – adding new contributions to this pattern's continuing tradition.

For information about entering the current year's contest write:

MAQS

P.O. Box 1540

Paducah, KY 42002-1540

The Sponsors

A special thanks goes to the corporations whose generous support has made this contest, exhibit, and book possible:

The Contest

This publication grows out of an annual international contest sponsored by the Museum of the American Quilter's Society. Entitled "New Quilts from Old Favorites," this contest encourages quiltmakers to develop innovative quilts using a different traditional pattern each year. The theme for 1996 was the traditional Ohio Star pattern, a long-time favorite of quilters.

The only design requirement for quilts entered in the contest was that the quilt be recognizable in some way as related to the Ohio Star pattern. The quilt also had to be a minimum of 50" in each dimension and not exceed 100" in any one dimension, and it had to be quilted. A quilt could only be entered by the person who made it, and had to have been completed after December 31, 1990. Many exciting interpretations of this traditional pattern were submitted by quilters from around the world. From these entries were selected the 18 quilts featured in both this publication and the traveling exhibition.

The Ohio Star pattern, which has long been a favorite with quilters, often bears other pattern names. Depending on color placement in the triangle areas, it can become Variable Star, Texas Star, and other patterns. Involving only two templates – a triangle and a square – its simple shapes allow for easy experimentation with coloration and actual fabrics. Set solid, exciting and varied overall designs can be planned. Isolated by sashing or alternate plain blocks, individual stars boldly shine.

Ohio Star

Contemporary quiltmakers were no less inspired than their predecessors by this pattern selected for the 1996 contest.

In some cases the quilts entered in this contest were projects that had already been underway at the time the contest was announced; in other cases they had already been completed.

On the other hand, a number of quilts entered in the competition were inspired by the contest theme. Some of the quilters commented that they had made Ohio Star quilts, but this was their first use of the pattern in an innovative way. This contest provided just the incentive they needed.

Several winners remarked that they have found the Ohio Star pattern interesting enough that they anticipate making other quilts based on this design. In this book you will find comments from each of the winners, illustrating the variety of experiences and reactions these individuals had to working with this popular traditional pattern.

Some of the quilters have retained much from the traditional design, modifying only slightly the pieced structure and usual use of the design. Other quilters have boldly moved in new directions, re-interpreting the design quite dramatically. The quilts are a wonderful reminder of the latitude that traditional patterns offer quiltmakers. These patterns are there to be followed to whatever degree the maker wishes. And regardless of the degree of modification, the results can be very spectacular.

The Winners

IZUMI TAKAMORI

Tokyo, Japan

CRYSTAL STAR

MAGGIE POTTER

Walnut Creek, California

STAR FIELD

SUE SPIGEL

Christchurch, New Zealand

WITHOUT ORANGE, THERE IS NO BLUE

GERTRUDE EMBREE & GAYLE WALLACE

Shreveport, Louisiana

OHIO LANDSCAPE

NANCY S. BROWN

Oakland, California

SOMETHING'S FISHY

And Their Quilts

FINALISTS

CORINNE APPLETON

JUDY BECKER

SHIRLEY ROBINSON DAVIS

DEANNA D. DISON

KEIKO GOKE

ELIZABETH HENDRICKS

GENE P. H. IVES

JOANNA JOHNSON

GERI KINNEAR

JANE LLOYD

LINDA D. Y. SOKALSKI

SUSAN STEIN

LAURA WASILOWSKI

CRYSTAL STAR

88" x 88", 1995

Cotton & acetate/rayon

Machine pieced, hand embroidered

& machine quilted

Izumi Takamori

TOKYO, JAPAN

MY QUILTMAKING

For years I experimented with knitting, embroidery, sewing, and making a wide variety of other needle art. Then 17 years ago I saw my first art quilt, and I began to take quilting classes to learn proper techniques. I studied for two years.

Creating quilts satisfies my urges to touch, collect, and experiment with many different kinds of fabric.

Last year I signed up for a class from Emiko Toda Loeb when she was teaching in Japan. She gave me an assignment to make an Eight-Point Star quilt. I have always loved star designs, and was inspired by the Ohio Star pattern, which many people love. I was able to complete CRYSTAL STAR before the end of the class, but it was only this year that I had time to add the embroidery.

I now have a quilt shop and work every day in the shop, which keeps me very busy. But I plan to continue to make quilts for my own satisfaction and also for entering into competitive quilt shows.

MY OHIO STAR QUILT

When I began CRYSTAL STAR, my Eight-Point Star assignment for Emiko Toda Loeb's class, I knew I wanted to make a white quilt with many kinds of white fabric, lace, and embroidery. Cotton, acetate/rayon, and cotton lace are all included in the top, which was constructed using fast machine-piecing techniques. The quilt was then machine quilted with metallic thread. Hand embroidery was added with cotton, polyester, and rayon threads, knitting yarn, and sashiko thread, a special cotton thread.

I worked with the Ohio Star pattern again, as back art planned for CRYSTAL STAR, but this Ohio Star design instead ended up on the front of a quilt I call "Puzzled Star." Both of these Ohio Star quilts were fun to make and exiting to finish. I like both of them, and would like the challenge of creating another design using the Ohio Star pattern.

> I hope looking at my quilt gives people ideas about how they could develop their own designs for quilts.

See page 68 for design insights.

15

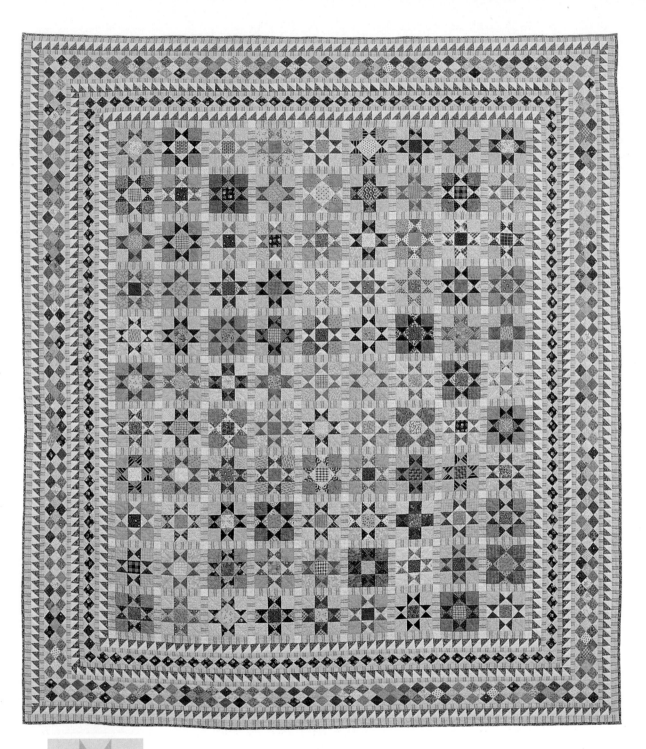

SECOND
PLACE

STAR FIELD

66" x 77", 1995

Cotton

Machine pieced & hand quilted

Maggie Potter

WALNUT CREEK, CA

MY QUILTMAKING

It was in 1983 that I began quilting, the year my first daughter was born. Prior to that I had been a weaver – and had also been very involved with surfing. I now have three daughters, ages 6, 9, and 12, and find I drive across town at least six times a day. But, being an artist, I will always find time to create because that is part of my life.

I have two close friends who know my work well, having seen it develop over the years. They cheer me on when I become tired and discouraged, and my husband Frank, is also very supportive. Years ago I had the opportunity to see the Esprit quilt collection in San Francisco, which was most inspiring.

STAR FIELD is my fifth quilt with an elaborate border – borders can be very tedious. I don't have a specific quilt in mind for my next project, but it probably won't have a border!

MY OHIO STAR QUILT

This quilt was made specially for the MAQS contest and was an exciting project. I have used the Ohio Star pattern only once before, but I enjoy making quilts with different star patterns, my favorite being the Evening Star, a Four-Patch design.

STAR FIELD consists of 99 Ohio Star blocks, each 4½", plus multiple borders. The back is also pieced – I always add extra unrelated squares to the back. The entire quilt has over 4,500 pieces, all tea-dyed. I like the subtle color combinations and the sashing fabric. I didn't want the sashing to stand out. I've found that the sashing can make or break a quilt.

I am very influenced by antique quilts. They have a great deal of character, and I enjoy the fact that they are not perfect. I don't worry about the points of stars being perfect or squares being exact. I am more concerned about the overall design. Antique quilts, with their imperfections, are wonderful.

Twelve years ago I had to convert my weaving studio into a nursery. Needing to continue to do something creative, I decided to make quilts – they didn't require a studio. I haven't woven since.

See page 78 for tips on adding borders.

WITHOUT ORANGE, THERE IS NO BLUE

70" x 70", 1995

Cotton patchwork fabric, cotton classic batting,

Madiera® embroidery thread

Machine pieced & quilted

Sue Spigel

CHRISTCHURCH, NEW ZEALAND

MY QUILTMAKING

I began making doll clothes on a sewing machine when I was four years old. I remember seeing quilts and hearing about family quilting bees held in Ontario before I was born, but it wasn't until I met Pat Cairns, from Vancouver, BC, who was visiting a friend in New Zealand, that I realized quilts could be made on the sewing machine.

When I stopped work as a speech therapist in 1983, in order to take care of my young children, I began quiltmaking to preserve my sanity. I began teaching almost immediately, and now own a patchwork shop in Christchurch, but still manage to make about six quilts a year, primarily for exhibitions.

I have to keep making new quilts because I have so many ideas of pattern, color, and design flying through my head. I enjoy the discipline of trying to incorporate successful qualities from previous quilts with some new idea.

MY OHIO STAR QUILT

This quilt was inspired by the MAQS contest. I read about it just after my daughter left home for college in the US and my husband went with her to help her get settled in. I was feeling rather empty – the contest provided a focus and a deadline.

Most of my quilts are based on some form of a traditional block, but I had never used an Ohio Star block. It proved to be an excellent design as it could be broken down into several different components, vertically, horizontally, and diagonally through which colors could be washed in different directions.

I worked in 4 x 4 units of stars, shading the background of each diagonally from dark to light. The patchwork was made without the use of templates and was machine pieced and free-machine quilted using predominately stipple quilting.

I love the way the stars are different even though there is an underlying rhythm to them. I would like to work with the block again to vary the position and the scale of various blocks.

I love to sit at my machine, enjoying the touch and look of fabrics as I stitch them together – and the excitement of discovering the pattern as it takes form

See page 101 for rotary cutting directions.

OHIO LANDSCAPE

78" x 63", 1995

Cotton fabrics, commercial & hand dyed,

hand printed, hand marbled

Machine pieced & machine quilted

Gertrude Embree & Gayle Wallace

Commentary by Gertrude Embree

SHREVEPORT, LA

MY QUILTMAKING

Gayle and I enjoy working together and look forward to collaborating again. I began quiltmaking in the early 1960's and made several bed quilts for my family in the 1970's but it wasn't until the late 1980's that I found my loom shoved in a corner while my fabric collection grew. Designing is always a struggle for me and self doubt is a gremlin I constantly fight. But I love to create, in quilting and as a closet cartoonist.

I choose to make quilts because I love their special surface texture and potential for creativity on a large scale. I also enjoy the community of creative people in the quilt world and their willingness to share their discoveries.

Gayle started quilting in 1985 and has since taught over 1,500 students, a number of whom have gone on to win awards. Gayle makes quilts to please herself. Seeing someone softly touch and appreciate the work that went into the making of a quilt is a great joy for her. It was Gayle who encouraged me to enter this quilt in the MAQS contest.

MY OHIO STAR QUILT

It was great fun to play with the Ohio Star, an old pattern I had worked with often in my weaving. I began the design on my computer using draw and paint software. Several quilts emerged from this computer play; however, a painting by Japanese artist Toshinobu Onosato inspired me to begin again. Using graph paper, I worked out the design. At the same time the quilt design was evolving, I was also having a lot of fun experimenting with fabric painting and printing.

The colors in the quilt represent the blues and greens of our beautiful earth which is the central sphere. Ohio itself is, of course, the large star within the sphere – blue for its great river. The woods and fields of my childhood home in southern Ohio are nested in the center. A scrap of my mother's dress is at the very heart. Farmlands surround the circle and corn stars symbolize the cities. Like many of my quilts, this is a Green Quilt, which carries a message of hope for the health of our planet. The machine quilting was done by Gayle, using a monofilament thread.

I first discovered the Ohio Star pattern in a piece of handwoven Swedish folk art and adapted it to my own weaving. When I moved on to quiltmaking, the star moved on with me.

Gertrude Embree (l) & Gayle Wallace (r)

See page 80 for design insights.

21

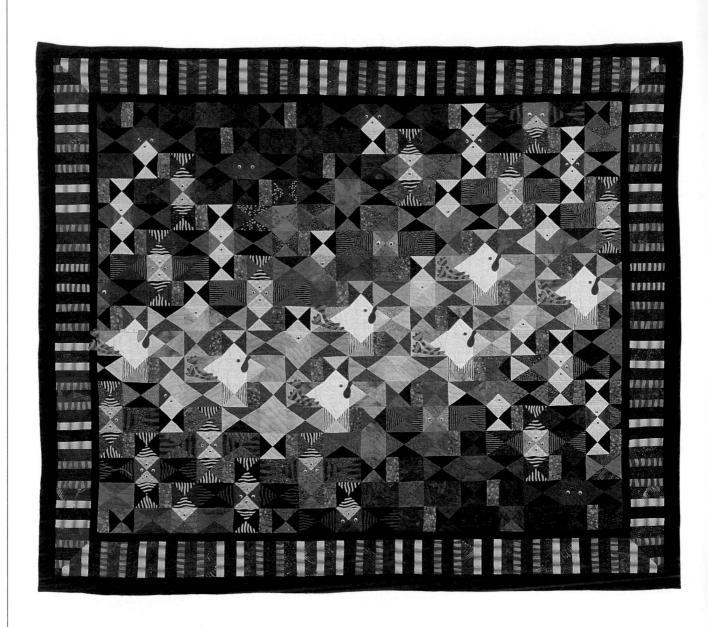

SOMETHING'S FISHY

64" x 54", 1995

Cotton

Machine pieced, hand appliquéd & hand quilted

Nancy S. Brown

OAKLAND, CA

MY QUILTMAKING

My mother is the person most responsible for my becoming a quiltmaker. She taught me to quilt in the early 1980's. She prefers traditional patterns, but encouraged me to develop my own designs. She also took me to quilt shows and lectures. Once she got me started it was very easy for me to become hooked.

SOMETHING'S FISHY may surprise people who know me because I usually make realistic appliqué animal quilts. This quilt is almost all pieced and the animals are fantasy beings. I also very rarely use red, orange, or yellow, so this quilt is a bit of a departure in that respect as well.

I make quilts because I enjoy everything associated with the process. I continue to make animal quilts because I love animals and think they ought to be celebrated. I plan to make animal quilts forever. Animals are an endless source of inspiration and enjoyment for me. I also hope to inject a little humor into my quilts, every now and then.

MY OHIO STAR QUILT

This quilt is based on the strange but true phenomenon known as the migration of the Pollo del Mar (chickens of the sea). This migration occurs deep in the ocean every spring, and it has been reported that when schools of other fish see this strange sight they stop in their tracks and form small discussion groups. Since this phenomenon has never been photographed, I thought it might be nice to represent it in a quilt.

The only animals I could design using the Ohio Star were fish, chickens, and lions. I couldn't figure out what to do with the lions, but I thought the chickens, which looked more like a strange type of chicken-fish, might look nice with the fish. I then designed a pattern with this unusual species swimming through a school of very startled fish. I elongated two sides of the Ohio Star pattern so most of the action would flow horizontally. I am pleased with the chickens of the sea, but less sure about the success of the chicken leg border. It's a bit loud, but this quilt is not subtle – it needs a wild border.

I had never used the Ohio Star pattern before, but had always admired it in quilts. I wanted to make a quilt for the MAQS contest, but only if I could figure a way to make it an animal quilt.

See page 81 for patterns.

ALL CATS GO TO HEAVEN

60" x 60", 1995

Cotton fabric & batting, various threads, buttons

Machine appliquéd, *broderie perse*,

hand beaded, machine pieced

Corinne Appleton

JACKSONVILLE, FL

MY QUILTMAKING

The impending birth of my first niece in 1987 found me working on something that resembled a quilt, and when my enthusiasm overflowed, I also made a Log Cabin throw. These two pseudo-quilts would have been my entire quilting legacy were it not for the unwavering support of my father.

People often seem to think my quilts spring to life easily and magically. They don't – there is often near agony involved in my quiltmaking, whether it is related to the message, the design, or the construction. ALL CATS GO TO HEAVEN was somewhat an exception, but I credit this to the fact that I had already spent a considerable amount of time exploring alternatives on the Electric Quilt 2® program.

Often women refer to their quilting as a hobby, sometimes as a passion, and only rarely as an obsession. I live, breathe, and dream quilts. I make quilts because I must. They are my voice.

MY OHIO STAR QUILT

I viewed the wonderful Log Cabin quilts in the 1995 MAQS contest and found myself intrigued with making an Ohio Star quilt for the 1996 contest. A new user of the Electric Quilt 2® computer design software, I began to experiment. My original EQ2 design has yet to be made, but with a stack of new fabrics I began rotary slicing and a different Ohio Star quilt emerged.

Comprised of nine stars that represent the nine lives that folklore has attributed to cats, this quilt celebrates the lives of five cats I had been mourning for many months. These stars shine in the heavenly garden where I envision my five cats gamboling happily. Of course, they are not alone in their feline heaven; there are many who have gone before them and they, too, are there.

"O heaven will not ever Heaven be Unless my cats are here with me," an epitaph from a pet cemetery, perfectly expresses my feelings and, I suspect, those of many fortunate enough to have known love from those wonderful bundles of fur.

ALL CATS GO TO HEAVEN seemed to help make itself, right down to the wonderful flying "angel" cat fabric that appeared in one of my favorite quilt shops the day before I needed it.

See page 88 for design tips.

AN OLD MASK

56" x 56", 1995

Drapery fabric, taffeta, cottons, chintz,
cotton batting

Machine pieced, hand & machine quilted

Judy Becker

NEWTON, MA

MY QUILTMAKING

I didn't know how to sew, but in 1973, armed with Beth Gutcheon's *The Perfect Patchwork Primer*, I made my first quilt block – an Ohio Star block. Six months and twenty pillows later (each made with a different block), I made my first bed quilt. Again it was an Ohio Star design.

When I began quilting I was the full-time director of a preschool, and a mother of two young children, which was also a full-time activity. In other words, my working and home life were basically chaotic. Quilting offered order, a creative outlet, and satisfaction for my obsessive tendencies.

In 1985 I left teaching to quilt full-time. I lecture, teach, and enjoy my solitary studio time. My husband is an amateur potter, and my daughter is a glassblower and high school art teacher, so my home environment is supportive of creativity. I also meet monthly with a critique group of six women, to share ideas and get feedback on works in progress.

MY OHIO STAR QUILT

For many years I have been developing my own contemporary designs. Some are linear, some fractured, architectural, abstract, or representational, but none are traditional. The challenge, therefore, in creating AN OLD MASK was to add my individual voice to a much loved old pattern.

I had packed a dozen fabrics and moved them with me to the beach for the summer. When color choices are severely limited, it can be strangely liberating. In the background, I incorporated a linear motif that I have used repeatedly in my work and utilized the star components for masks. I have been developing a series of self-portrait quilts using masks and felt they might add a jolt of new life to an otherwise static composition.

I never respond to contests with a theme – my mind instantly goes blank. So much for that word "never." The Ohio Star theme brought over me a wave of nostalgia. The first quilt block I had ever made was an Ohio Star block.

See page 84 for patterns.

O-GEE OHIO

69½" x 52", 1995

Cotton, gold metallic thread

Machine pieced, appliqué, machine
embroidered, machine quilted

Shirley Robinson Davis

PRESCOTT, AZ

MY QUILTMAKING

In 1987 I started making traditional quilts. I was living on a ranch in northern Nevada and was talked into taking a quilt class. From then on I knew quilting was something I wanted to do. The first quilts I made were scrap quilts, and I continue to make them for myself. I teach machine quilting and quiltmaking in a shop in Prescott, have taught workshops to several groups, and always have several quilts in the making.

Outside of taking two quilt classes, I have learned on my own, reading many excellent books and experimenting with different methods. My motto is "Never be afraid to fail; you may come up with something wonderful." I love experimenting with different fabrics and techniques. People who knew me earlier would probably be surprised to learn that I am a quiltmaker because I was always on a horse, drawing and painting, or taking photographs. People are surprised that I sit still long enough to finish a quilt.

MY OHIO STAR QUILT

My quilt O-GEE OHIO was made specially for the MAQS contest. I love the Ohio Star pattern, and I had some wonderful batiks I wanted to use in a special quilt. I would like people to look into the ogee centers and view them as windows into life or the soul of the quilt. This quilt took on a life of its own after I started the piecing; it told me what to do. I would also like people to enjoy the celebration of color.

I am especially pleased with this quilt because the design is totally mine. It is not related directly to anyone else's work. There is always something I might change about a quilt were I to do it again, but on the whole I'm pleased with the way this one turned out. I plan to keep working with the Ohio Star pattern, in fact I have a number of blocks finished for a scrap plaid quilt using the pattern.

I have worked with the Ohio Star pattern many times before, but always in a traditional manner and always in scrap variations. Born in Ohio, I have an emotional tie with the design.

See page 62 for tips on making stretched blocks

RED SKY AT NIGHT

52" x 66", 1995

Cotton fabric, cotton batting

Machine pieced & hand quilted

FINALIST

Deanna D. Dison

SPEARSVILLE, LA

MY QUILTMAKING

I learned to quilt in the 1950's as a teenager. My mother made quilts so I had watched the construction process as a girl. After I married in 1960 I began to raise a family and make easy traditional quilts.

I went to college from 1977 to 1983 and received a bachelor's degree in landscape design and a master's degree in botany, which broadened my knowledge of color and design and made me appreciate nature more. I didn't get serious about quiltmaking until 1990.

Most people think of me as a person who could not sit still long enough to make a quilt. They would be surprised to know that I make about a dozen quilts (six large and six small) each year.

I make quilts because I love to do it, and I make time to do what I love. Since January 1995 I have used my computer to design three quilts, and all please me. I can't wait to use it more.

MY OHIO STAR QUILT

At the 1995 AQS Quilt Show I purchased a quilt software program for my computer. Back home I chose the Ohio Star pattern as a simple block to practice with. With this quilt I learned the ins and outs of the program. I found I enjoyed using the computer software in the design process because it made everything work out more quickly. I was able to color at a faster pace, move blocks more easily, and re-size blocks or the quilt with just a click.

This quilt is about when the sun goes down and day turns into night – when we have ended a part of our life that we can't redo, whether it be good or bad. The name came from the saying "Red sky at night, sailor's delight. Red sky in the morning, sailor take warning." I hope all of our nights are a delight. I originally made a quilt named "Ideas" for this contest, but was unhappy with it, so I made this one, which I don't believe I could have made without the computer.

I love traditional designs and I also love the challenge of trying to use them in a non-traditional way.

See page 93 for patterns.

MY OHIO STAR

60" x 62", 1995

Cotton

Machine pieced, hand embroidered

& machine quilted

Keiko Goke

SENDAI, MIYAGI, JAPAN

MY QUILTMAKING

I have been working with patchwork quilting ever since I saw several projects in a Japanese interior design magazine more than 20 years ago. In those days, there was hardly any literature on quilting in my country. I would look through magazines to find one patchwork-looking project and then add the clipping to the scrapbook I used as a reference book. It was almost impossible to find quilt batting in those days, so I would use towels or flannel.

I founded Quilt Circle Kei in 1979. Ever since, I have held classes twice a week in my home for my 30 students. We often have coffee and cake and almost always have a wonderful time quilting! When I started quilting, I was very shy. Quilting has opened up an entirely new world. I have traveled in Japan and abroad to teach and exhibit my quilts, and I have met many wonderful people and quilts. I look forward most to the new experiences that lie before me. A big thanks goes to quilting!

MY OHIO STAR QUILT

Since the time I returned home from Paducah in May 1995, I had been contemplating what kind of Ohio Star quilt I would make. As the contest's title indicates, a traditional-looking quilt would not work. I drew many sketches of original Ohio Star blocks – my very own Ohio Stars. I then selected one and used it as the basis for a drawing of five Ohio Stars, made on a large sheet of paper the same size as the finished quilt. With their elongated sides and distorted shapes, my quilt's Ohio Stars were much freer than those in traditional blocks.

When I first encountered patchwork quilting, I made sampler quilts and bags using the Ohio Star pattern; however, this is the first time I had ever made a quilt just using this one pattern. I hope to make into quilts some of the other Ohio Star sketches I drew while planning my contest quilt.

> I have always felt sorry for the Ohio Star pattern because it is almost always fit into a square or rectangle. It always looks cramped in such a confined space. I like to think my distorted stars are stretching and feeling free and easy.

See page 64 for tips on drawing designs freehand

A LONG WAY FROM CINCINNATI

52" x 52", 1995

Cotton fabrics, rayon braids, cotton & rayon threads

Machine piecing, machine appliqué, machine quilting

(free motion) & couching

Elizabeth Hendricks

SEATTLE, WA

MY QUILTMAKING

I began quilting four and a half years ago, with the birth of my nephew Joshua. In my former life I was in product development and marketing. For almost 20 years my career was so consuming that I had little time for artistic pursuits.

I began quilting at home, which for me is a house barge on Seattle's Lake Union. I had a crazy way of working in the confines of the aft cabin, and varied my methods depending upon how much the water might be moving.

After quilting during the storms of February 1993, I decided to get a little studio on land, a place where the walls stayed still, and the floors didn't dance. I now have a little studio which is just a walk up the lake and across a drawbridge.

As a hobby I also fly small planes, so the designs or quilting lines in many of my pieces have a sense of floating. What I am working toward in quilting is for my command of technique to catch-up with my imagination, to then see what emerges.

MY OHIO STAR QUILT

I had not worked with the Ohio Star pattern before, and was intrigued by its possibilities. I used to do business in Ohio and also now associate Ohio with quilt national and Nancy Crow's symposium, so the state has very positive associations.

I broke the Ohio Star design into two grids – the lower composed of horizontal and vertical lines, and the upper one of diagonals. I then pieced the lower Nine-Patch grid in cold colors, and the upper in hot. When putting them back together, however, I couldn't see one grid for the other since the fabrics were opaque. I decided to cut curls through the layer of diagonals, so that once they were overlaid, the eye would connect the lines of the star. After quilting, I couched rayon braid to highlight the base structure of the stars.

I hope people enjoy tracing the straight edged star within the colors of the curvilinear shapes and the secondary pattern (emphasized by the yellow wiggly shapes). I meant this piece to be up-beat and happy, and hope that optimism is conveyed.

I was inspired and intrigued by the thought of making an Ohio Star quilt. I have done very little traditional block construction, so it was an enjoyable departure for me.

Photo by Chris Bennion

See page 66 for couching techniques.

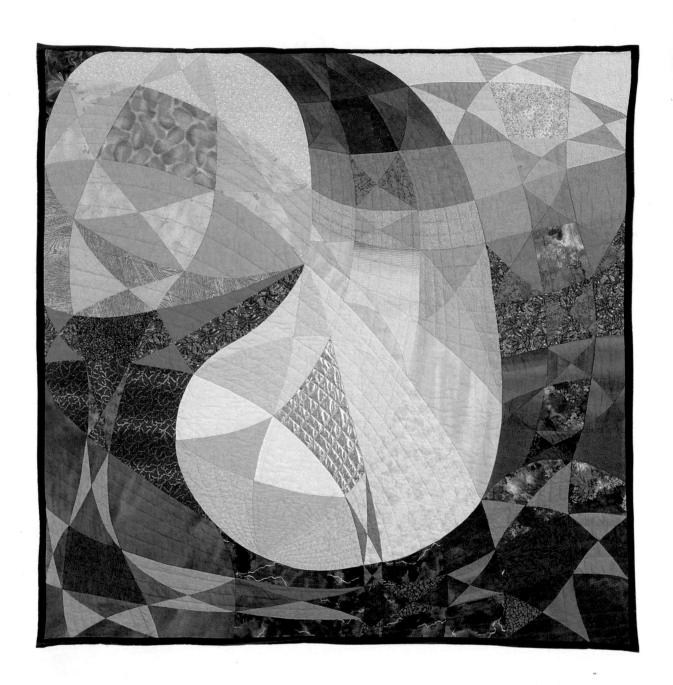

WHY-O-WHY OHIO

60" x 60", 1995

Cotton fabric, gold lamé, & wool batting

Hand pieced & hand quilted

Gene P. H. Ives

ALEXANDRIA, VA

MY QUILTMAKING

After nearly 30 years as a full-time commercial artist, I took up quilting in 1991. My local quilt guild guided me into lessons and gave lots of loving assistance. Needless to say, I'm hopelessly addicted. It never ceases to amaze me at the imagination and the difference in interpretations shown by each quilter.

Creating things has always been part of me from as far back as I can remember. When I first started school as a little girl, our school bus was a covered wagon pulled by two mules. In my teens I was evacuated out of the Philippine Islands just ahead of the invading Japanese in 1941. I learned to fly a plane long before I learned to drive a car.

My quilting is forever a challenge to try to please the viewer. One person who I find most inspirational is Anne Oliver, who is in our quilt bee. She encourages me to strive to do my best, not to be satisfied with just OK, but to have the courage to pull out those not-quite-right stitches and try again. She is surely my guiding "star."

MY OHIO STAR QUILT

The Ohio Star block was one of the first I ever learned to piece. I do not have strong associations other than my intense interest in old patterns and their history. The idea for this quilt was strictly my own – a sort of doodle. I then worked out the design through a series of thumbnail sketches. The quilt consists of 11 Ohio Stars that have been punched and squeezed, stretched and pulled.

What pleases me most about the quilt are the secondary patterns that developed because of the color placements – the big fish on the left side standing on his tail, the palm tree on the right, surprises like these. I hope viewers enjoy the flow of colors, one into the other and the movement caused by the quilting, which encourages your eyes to travel over the surface and back again.

It was the MAQS contest that inspired this quilt. The challenge was to use the Ohio Star and somehow make it different. It's a delight to work with the block – to watch how color changes can result in additional patterns.

See page 74 for design tips.

GOTTA DANCE

59" x 79", 1995

Hand-dyed & commercial cottons, silks, lamé

Machine pieced & machine quilted

FINALIST

JoAnna Johnson

CARBONDALE, IL

MY QUILTMAKING

I began quilting in 1985, because of childhood memories of a Grandmother's Flower Garden quilt. My mother read to my sister and me every night, and she often fell asleep before we did. We would then look at the quilt's patches and make up stories about them.

I do not have drawing talent but I love working with color, so fabric is a perfect medium for me. Many of my non-quilting friends and family still don't think of quiltmaking as an art form. In their eyes, quilts are for beds. The idea of telling a story with a quilt or making one to express an emotion is a surprise to them.

Quilts can be fulfilling in many ways: through their ties to the past – comfort, security, love, warmth – and through their promise for the future – anything is possible. I love quilting because it lets me express myself. Quilting gives me many ways to explore who I am, and it fills me with good feelings.

MY OHIO STAR QUILT

This quilt developed in my mind over a two-year period. The beginning came with a comment made by Judi Warren in a Star Garden class at MAQS. She said, "You could have a 'Star Garden' in outer space." Later I was watching *Sesame Street* with my son. One segment was a story about the man-in-the-moon being lonely and visiting earth to dance in earth's garden. Technically the quilt is about the man-in-the-moon visiting earth to dance in earth's star gardens, but most of all, I want people to know it's about joy and being happy.

Designing the quilt, I divided the earth along latitude and longitude lines, and Ohio Stars seemed perfect for the sections. I knew I wanted string piecing between the moon and the earth and the trail, so I took Caryl Bryer Fallert's string piecing class, to help me understand how my idea could be accomplished. My new skills were used to execute my idea. I like the overall impression and enjoy the fact that the longer you look at my quilt the more interesting it becomes.

The first thing people say when they find out you're a quiltmaker is, "You must be very patient." I'm not. But the joy of the finished project and the process of completing it make the effort worthwhile.

See page 70 for tips on drafting skewed Ohio Stars

RIVERS OF DESTINY

54" x 54", 1995

Cottons, some African cottons, beads,
decorative threads

Bonded, hand beaded, machine pieced
& machine quilted

Geri Kinnear

HINSDALE, IL

MY QUILTMAKING

My first quilt was a baby quilt, based on an idea from a magazine. Then I began taking classes, attending conferences, and reading every book and magazine I could get my hands on! Reading about traditional quilts, I became fascinated with the history of women in America. I collected old quilts and gave lectures about quilting and women's history. I also used quilts to teach my students about early America.

My mother fostered my love for reading, and encouraged my interest in all forms of sewing. She taught me to take pride in my work and find joy in my creativity. She died long before I became a quilter, and I'm very envious of the mothers and daughters I know who share this interest together.

My husband is my best friend and critic and has supervised the building of two studios for me. I have been working on a series of memory quilts, and have several more in the "thinking" stage.

MY OHIO STAR QUILT

I had no clear plan for using these African fabrics until I watched news of the first democratic election in South Africa. The lines of African people waiting to vote appeared to be rivers of human beings stretching far into the horizon. As teacher of young children, I am always drawn to graphic illustrations of complex issues. The desire for freedom and change was so clearly communicated by the lines of voters.

As an artist, I wished to record these moments of joy, optimism, and hope. I chose the Ohio Star as a dramatic symbol of light and hope, and graduated the size of the stars to represent the rivers of people waiting to change their own destiny. It seemed natural to use African fabric for the stars.

My first Ohio Star block was made in a sampler quilt class which I took in 1980. We drafted our own templates, and my Ohio Star block never came out correctly. The ends of the points were sewn into the sashing! I'm fond of the Ohio Stars in RIVERS OF DESTINY they dance across the surface of the quilt, and have all their points!

This quilt began with a collection of African fabrics. Once I had decided to use the concept of rivers, it was easy to visualize Ohio Stars disappearing into the background, representing freedom from oppression.

Photo by James B. Tweedle

See page 105 for patterns

STAR LIGHT, STAR BRIGHT

50" x 50", 1995

Cotton/polyester blends

Strip piecing over paper

Jane Lloyd

BALLYMAEN, CO. ANTRIM, NORTHERN IRELAND

MY QUILTMAKING

I started quiltmaking in 1977 when I saw a quilt in a magazine and decided to make one. I had been to art college and worked in different mediums, but I found that this was a perfect medium for me. I used to do it all by hand because I had no confidence on the machine. My friends kept telling me that I could make more quilts if I used the machine, so I practiced and eventually got better. I have found a way of being as accurate as when hand sewing, by sewing over papers, and now I have several machines and an industrial one as well!

I belong to the Northern Ireland Patchwork Guild, which meets once a month, and also belong to a small group called Off Cuts which also meets on regular basis. This small group is great because we all help each other, with everything from taking out basting stitches to giving encouragement.

I continue to work on quilts, and enjoy the challenge of completing work for special shows and contests. I like working to dates – it motivates me.

MY OHIO STAR QUILT

My quilt was inspired by the MAQS contest. I get an idea in my head, think about it for some time, and then begin before I've finished the entire design. The design grows along the way. I knew I wanted to incorporate a large star within the nine blocks, but until the very end I didn't know how. I didn't want it to show up too much. I wanted people to look into the quilt and find the star.

I wanted to blend colors through the quilt diagonally. I am extremely fond of strips, which offer a good way of blending colors; they always seem to come into my quilts in some form, straight or curved. I find endless possibilities through strips. My three daughters, ages 16, 14, and 12, help me with design and color. They are very critical, and also have great ideas and inspire me.

It is always a challenge to work with a theme – you end up doing things you might not have done. It's good for the brain and makes you think of how you can change the traditional design, giving it your individual style.

IN THE BEGINNING

60" diameter, 1995

Cotton fabrics & polyester batting

Machine pieced & machine quilted

Linda D. Y. Sokalski

FLAT ROCK, NC

MY QUILTMAKING

Though both of my grand-mothers were avid quiltmakers and quilting bees were common in my family, I was generally shooed me away from the quilt-ing frame, so I became a knitter and embroiderer instead. My engineering career gave me the opportunity for considerable international travel, and I used those opportunities to study, write articles, and teach a num-ber of ethnic techniques.

The event most responsible for my becoming involved in quiltmaking was corporate downsizing in the telephone industry. In September 1992, as I was sitting in my office ponder-ing a very uncertain future, an image flashed through my mind which seemed more suited to a quilt than to embroidery. The result was my first quilt, which featured cyanotype prints of cor-porate executives bordered with short-circuited twisted pair tele-phone wire.

My husband and I are now both happily retired and view downsizing as the best thing that ever happened to us.

MY OHIO STAR QUILT

IN THE BEGINNING express-es the wonder of the creation of the universe. It has always fasci-nated me that as quilters we cre-ate similarly, beginning without form, separating the darkness from the light, and assembling the whole in a strikingly ordered process. If only we could finish on the sixth day!

Use of the Ohio Star block in this quilt about the creative process was particularly impor-tant, since my creative process is strongly influenced by my own Ohio Star, my Cleveland-born-and-bred husband, Ron.

I set out to achieve curved shapes and motion using only straight line piecing and I believe that these objectives were suc-cessful. I hope people viewing this quilt will recognize that most traditional square blocks can be drafted in non-right-angled quadrilaterals, often with very interesting results.

The most difficult aspect of developing this quilt was being limited to colors available in commercial fabrics. If I were to begin again, I would dye or over dye at least some of the fabrics.

> The Ohio Star has wonderful potential because of its strong vertical, horizontal, and diagonal lines, any of which can predominate depending upon use of color and value.

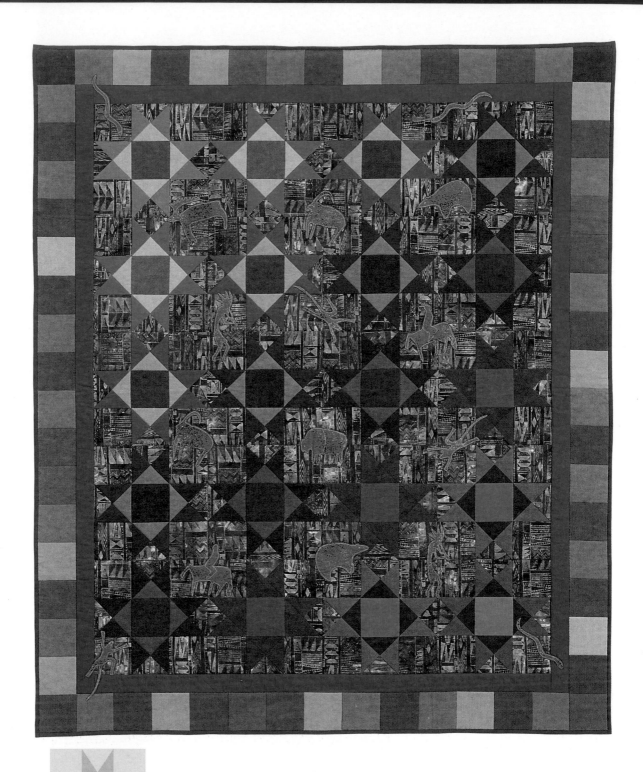

JOURNEY

60" x 72", 1995

Hand-dyed & commercial cotton

Machine pieced, raw-edge machine

appliquéd & machine quilted

Susan Stein

ST. PAUL, MN

MY QUILTMAKING

I began quilting in 1977 and have since worked for several publishers, taught classes, made commissioned quilts, made about 300 other quilted pieces, written a book, and owned two quilt shops – one in the early eighties and a second which opened in November 1995.

My mother was an occasional sewer and knitter and so got me started in crafts. Maybe fabric itself is the one thing that could be "blamed" for my current obsession with quilting. My husband's obsession with trains helps immensely to justify any level of activity I might pursue in quilting. My children grab any quilt that has served its purpose for teaching or publication so the inventory stays manageable.

My store is at the top of the list for projects – I always need samples for classes and patterns. Since the store is contemporary in focus I can have fun making samples using exciting fabrics and embellishments.

MY OHIO STAR QUILT

The pattern for the quilt was inspired by the MAQS contest, but the hand-dyed fabric bundle and commercial batik used had been "incubating" in my fabric cupboard for a couple of years.

I often work with dyed gradations so this was a natural way to approach the Ohio Star. As the design progressed, the wonderful interaction of the colors on the design wall inspired me to move away from my original concept of using a lot of appliqué over the stars. I instead used smaller motifs in the background areas.

The Ohio Star pattern often appears in my work with sampler quilts, but it is not a pattern that I had ever used for whole quilts. After completing this quilt, though, I can see other possibilities for using the stars as a "floating" element over an interesting background and for creating variations in the stars' centers.

It is my great desire to create new designs and interpret old ones in new ways that keeps me always in the process of making two or three different quilts.

See page 98 for complete instructions.

OHIO STAR: THANKS TO LENORE

50" x 53", 1995

Textile ink, dye, Silknoil, pearl cotton thread, cotton batting

Hand stamped design with textile ink & hand-dyed threads

couched to form star; machine pieced & machine quilted

Laura Wasilowski

ELGIN, IL

MY QUILTMAKING

In 1990 I was completing an MA in fiber and fabric, with an emphasis on surface design. I had begun my own company, Kaleidoscope Clothing, and was selling silk scarves and jackets to boutiques. A neighbor invited me to a lecture by Caryl Fallert and I was inspired. About this time I also met Melody Johnson, who made me realize my jacket scraps might be used in quilts.

In May 1992 I made my first quilt, and by the fall 1992 Melody and I had formed our company ARTFABR!K and were selling our hand-dyed fabrics to quiltmakers. By early 1995 I was concentrating on creating hand-dyed fabrics and narrative quilts.

My husband and children are very supportive of ARTFABR!K and my quiltmaking. They encourage me and, most importantly, provide me with humorous story ideas for quilts – like my current idea for a quilt called "Louise Learns to Juggle: Age 13 and Well Balanced." In the quilt will be my daughter Louise's hands juggling a cat, a pitcher of orange juice, and a bowling ball. The girl has talent.

MY OHIO STAR QUILT

Several events inspired this quilt. First, the MAQS contest was a challenge. I'm not a traditional quilter but have always admired the beauty and skill in traditional pieced quilts. Second, I had been teaching surface design techniques (stamping, silk screen printing, and painting on fabric). The purpose of the classes was to introduce quiltmakers to the art of printing their own fabrics.

One of the techniques I taught was the mono-print, a stamping method perfected by quiltmaker and surface design artist, Lenore Davis. The third event that triggered this quilt was the death of Lenore Davis in 1995. Although I never met her, her work has influenced me greatly.

I've never worked with the Ohio Star pattern before. I generally design my own quilt patterns and print and dye my own fabrics and threads. I like the idea of telling stories of my life, usually humorous or whimsical. I may again use a traditional block in an upcoming quilt, but it would probably be painted rather than pieced.

I have only made two quilts using traditional piecework. I'm not very good at following instructions, drawing a straight line, or being accurate. Rather than fight my own short comings, I work within them, designing my own patterns.

See page 61 for tips on mono-printing designs

49

Ohio Star Patterns

Included in this section are full templates for the traditional Ohio Star pattern in 13 sizes. Select the size most appropriate for your fabrics and project plans and try your own hand at this popular pattern.

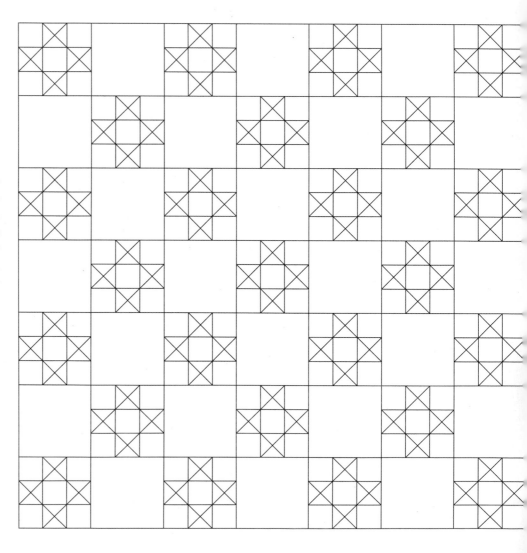

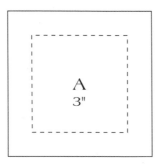

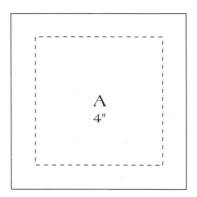

A
3"

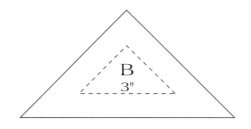

B
3"

A
4"

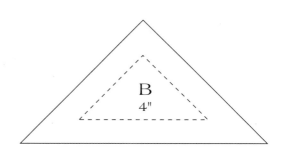

B
4"

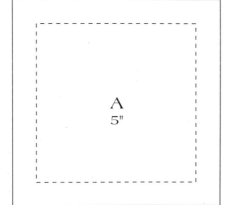

A
5"

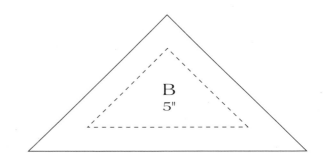

B
5"

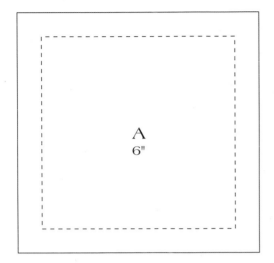

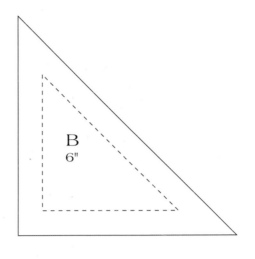

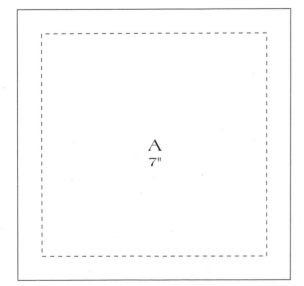

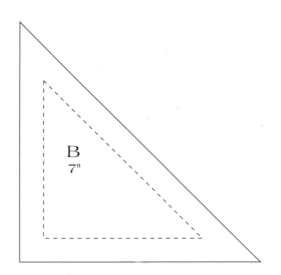

10", 11" BLOCK PATTERNS

¼" seam allowance included.

A
10"

B
10"

A
11"

B
11"

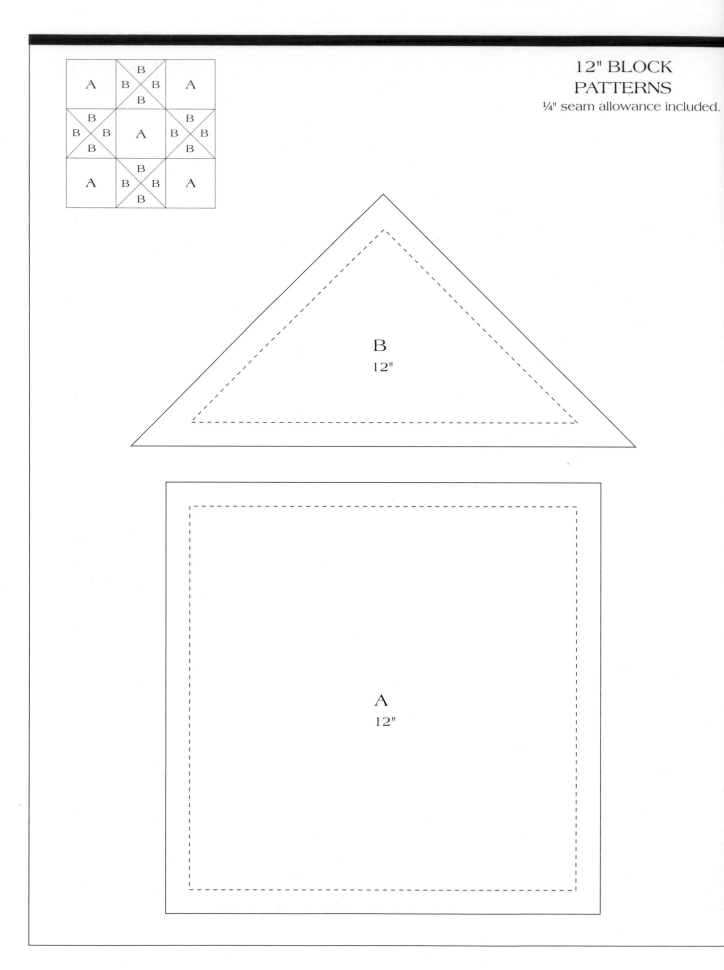

B
12"

A
12"

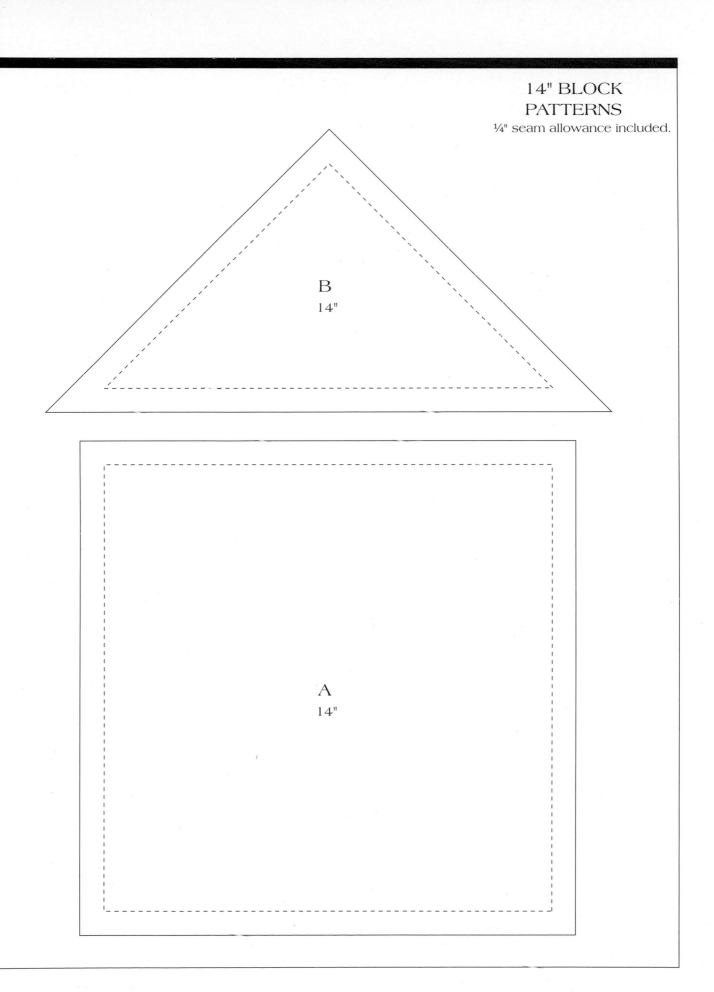

B
14"

A
14"

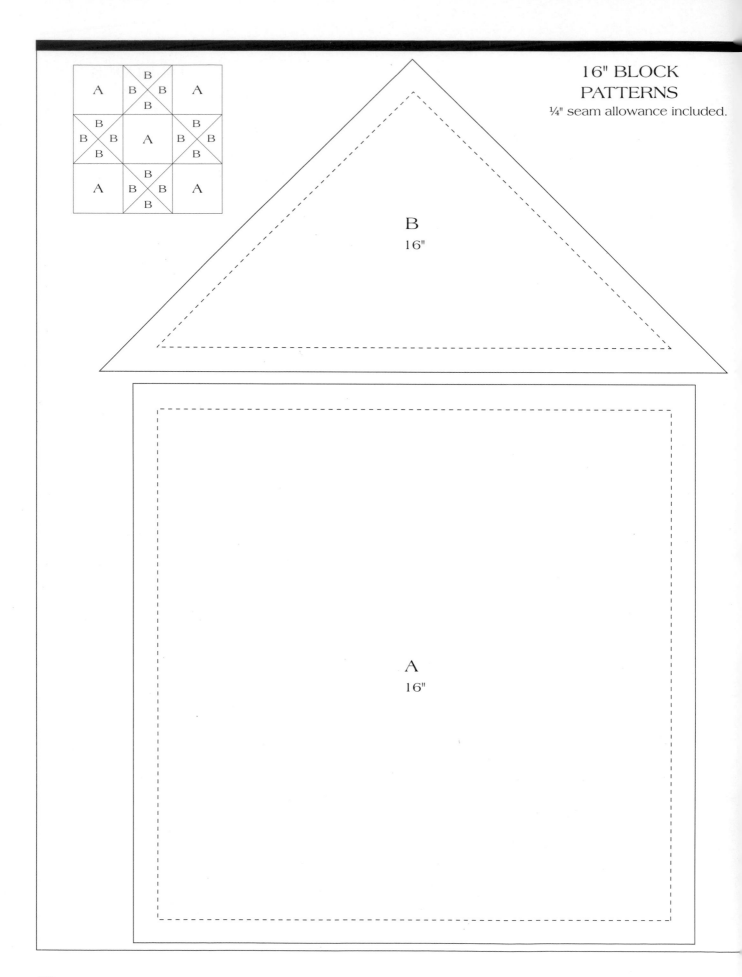

B
16"

A
16"

A
18"

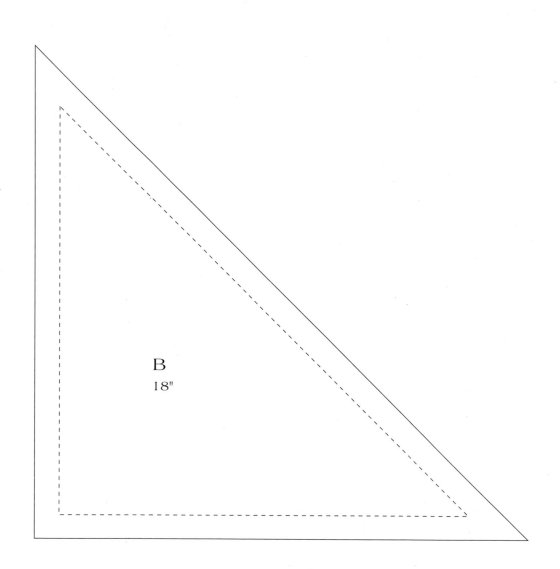

B
18"

Working with the Design

MONO-PRINTING DESIGNS
BY LAURA WASILOWSKI

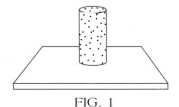

FIG. 1

The designs on my quilt OHIO STAR, THANKS TO LENORE were stamped with a non-toxic, water based, opaque textile ink on black silk noil. The stamping technique is called mono-printing. Mono-printing was perfected by artist, Lenore Davis, who created complex, pictorial fabrics with this simple technique.

To mono-print a fabric you need three tools:

- a stamp made from a flat, non-porous surface
- a paint or foam brush
- a pencil eraser

The stamp I used for my project was made from a square of clear, smooth plexi-glass. I attached a cork to one side of the plexi-glass with hot glue to form a handle (Fig. 1).

To mono-print your fabric, brush the textile ink onto the flat stamp with the foam brush (Fig. 2). Using the eraser of a pencil,

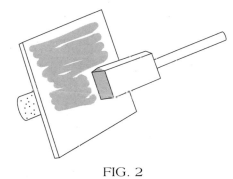

FIG. 2

draw designs into the textile ink on the stamp (Fig. 3). Carefully place the stamp and ink on the fabric and press firmly. Re-load the stamp with ink, draw your design with the eraser, stamp and repeat.

Some further tips:

- Practice stamping on scrap fabric first.

- If you are printing letters, you will have to draw them reversed on your stamp.

- Plan where you will place the stamp on the fabric. For instance, you may want to mark a grid on the fabric to follow before stamping.

- Be sure to follow the manufacturer's directions for setting the textile ink. Most inks are set with an iron or by placing printed fabrics in a dryer. Tools and hands clean up with warm water.

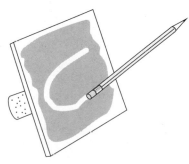

FIG. 3

MAKING STRETCHED BLOCKS
BY SHIRLEY ROBINSON DAVIS

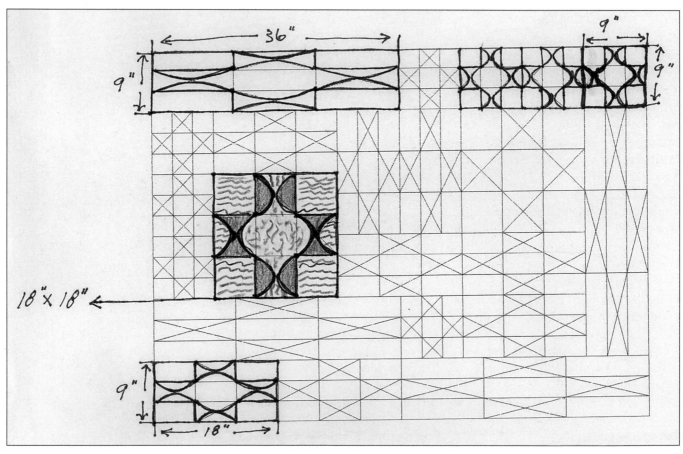

ABOVE: *Sketches for O-GEE-OHIO blocks*
PAGE 63, TOP: *The finished quilt*

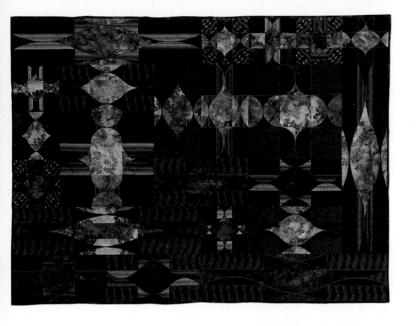

To create my quilt O-GEE-OHIO, shown left, I used four sizes of blocks: 9" x 9", 9" x 18", 9" x 36", and 18" x 18". I also altered the shape of individual pieces as well as the shape of the blocks, using rounded points instead of straight ones.

These stretched blocks were first created on the computer, but the actual patterns were drawn on graph paper, using a flexible curve.

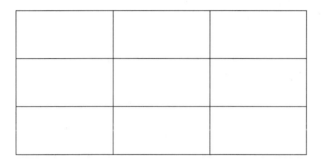

To create each block, I first stitched a Nine-Patch of squares or rectangles.

Then I cut two different shapes for adding to the Nine-Patch to make the points.

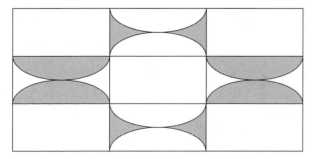

Next I used a paper-backed fusible web to fuse the points on.

To finish the blocks, I used a decorative stitch (cross stitch) on my sewing machine to go over the edges of the fused pieces.

DRAWING DESIGNS FREEHAND
BY KEIKO GOKE

MY OHIO STAR

When I design quilts, I try not to confine the pattern I'm working with, in this case the Ohio Star pattern, in a square or rectangle. I usually draw the design freehand on a sheet of paper that is the finished size of the quilt.

For the Ohio Star quilt, I drew several drawings freehand and chose one for my quilt. Shown right are several of my designs. They could all be adapted to any size quilt. The quilt that I made, shown left, involves many big pieces. Therefore, I have strip-pieced or crazy quilt-pieced the larger pieces. However, if the finished quilt is smaller than 40" x 40", the larger pieces in these designs could be made from just one piece of fabric.

FREEHAND OHIO STAR DRAWINGS

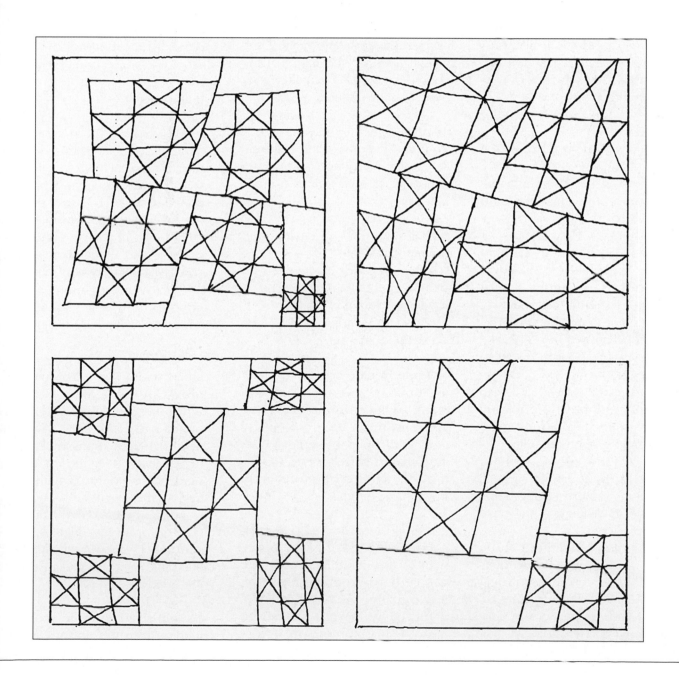

COUCHING TECHNIQUES FOR QUILTS
BY ELIZABETH HENDRICKS

Couching is a type of embellishment traditionally used by hand embroiderers. Careful spiralling stitches are used to lay thick threads or decorative braids on the surface, often creating lovely curving designs.

Today, couching lends itself beautifully to contemporary quiltmaking. By adapting this method to the machine, one can easily embellish with decorative threads, braids, yarns, or ribbons. These can be used to outline appliquéd shapes, cover raw edges, enhance major design elements, or create an element of line. The possibilities and variations are endless.

In A LONG WAY FROM CINCINNATI machine couching is used in two ways. One is to enhance shape, by outlining some of the appliqués. The other is to emphasize a line element in the block design. Couching braid in the original Ohio Star pattern subtly helps the eye to distinguish the base pattern.

Machine couching can be done on the top, prior to quilting, but this can make quilting challenging. It can also be added later as part of the quilting process. By adding it last,

couching can help to integrate the machine quilting lines, while adding texture to the quilted surface. I also like the effect of the couched threads or braids sinking more into the surface.

TECHNIQUE:

To add a decorative thread, braid or yarn to the quilted surface (for simplicity, I'll refer to it as a braid) you will need:

■ a large-eyed hand needle
■ a marking chalk
■ a zigzag sewing machine
■ an open foot for the machine
■ a full bobbin, and a matching cotton, rayon, or metallic thread for the top.

1. First, decide where to place the braid, and draw a line with chalk. Make sure the beginning and end of the line are clearly indicated. Do not attempt to pin the braid in place or pre-cut it to length, as both actions may thwart your efforts.

2. Thread the braid onto a large-eyed hand needle. At the beginning of the chalk line, poke the needle down from the top at an angle to the back (Fig A). The angle of the needle should be almost horizontal, to leave

approximately 1" of braid buried in the batting. Remove the needle from the braid and pull the other end of the braid forward so just a small tail is left on the quilt's back.

3. Set your machine for short straight stitches. Place your quilt under the machine, centering it where the couching braid appears, and hand lower the needle so it pierces the braid at its center (Fig. B). Lower your presser foot, and make two or three small stitches forward, then back stitch to the beginning. These stitches will hold the braid in place, and keep it from slipping.

4. Now set the machine zigzag stitch width just wider than the braid, so it goes into the fabric without catching the braid on either side. Slightly loosen the upper thread tension. Lay the braid down over the chalk line, working just four to five inches in front of the foot (Fig. C), and slowly zigzag the braid into place (Fig. D). The open foot allows you to see exactly where the needle is stitching, helping you to control the braid placement.

5. Stop stitching when about four inches from the finish. Carefully

measure your braid, allowing at least three extra inches beyond the end of the design. Cut the braid off, and thread it through the hand needle. Then carefully needle it through the top and batting at a horizontal angle toward you and out the quilt's back. Again leave about a 1" tail buried in the batting. Pull the braid taut, from beneath, then resume zigzagging to the design's end.

6. At the end, change the machine setting to a straight stitch, and back stitch several small stitches through the center of the braid to secure it.

7. Remove the quilt from the machine. Pull sewing threads to the back, knot, and with a hand needle bury the thread ends. Pull the couching braid tail taut from the back, and clip close to the surface. The braid tail will disappear into the quilt. With a fingernail scratch the hole in the cloth closed.

Once you are comfortable machine couching, you can begin to couch multiple braids beside one another, and create grids or wonderful curvilinear shapes. The possibilities are many. Enjoy.

A.

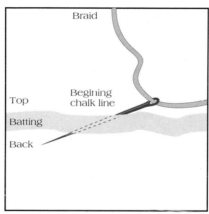

Side view – needling couching braid through at beginning.

B.

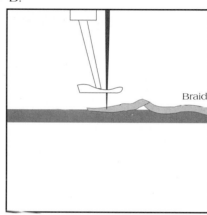

Hand lower the needle to pierce the braid at its center.

C.

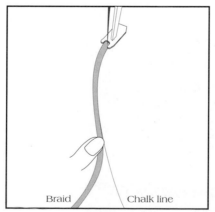

Lay the braid over the chalk line several inches at a time ahead of stitching.

D.

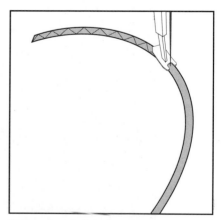

Zigzag close to the edges.

DESIGNING "CRYSTAL STAR"
BY IZUMI TAKAMORI

CRYSTAL STAR (top), and PUZZLED STAR (bottom)

In Emiko Toda Loeb's workshops I developed the design for CRYSTAL STAR (right). As you'll note from comparing it with the photo of the finished quilt (top left), I made a few changes when I actually made the quilt. Variations in the amount of contrast between star and background fabrics also make some stars and star parts much more visible than others in the final quilt.

While working on this quilt I planned a second Ohio Star design for the back, but this design eventually became a second Ohio Star quilt instead, PUZZLED STAR, shown bottom left. It is possible to create many new designs working with a traditional pattern like the Ohio Star.

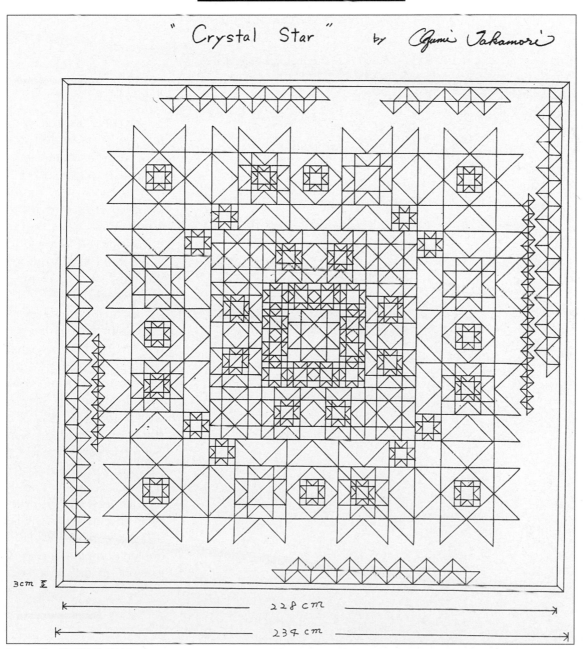

"Crystal Star" by Izumi Takamori

3cm

228 cm

234 cm

Layout for CRYSTAL STAR

DRAFTING SKEWED OHIO STARS
BY JOANNA JOHNSON

FIG. 1

GOTTA DANCE was pieced in four sections: moon, space, trail, and earth. I wanted the earth and the moon to be pieced in a similar way because they represent similar elements and they need to stand apart from the space and trail elements. I chose to fill them with Ohio Stars, to represent "star gardens" and to fit the theme of the contest.

In order to know what size each star would be, I realized I needed to draft my rough design (Fig. 1) full-size. Using several sheets of drafting velum taped together and tacked to a large wall, I used an 8½" x 11" transparency of my drawing on an overhead projector to transfer my design. Once I had traced the design onto the velum, I moved it to the floor and marked all the main design lines with a ruler and a fine-line black marker. With my design complete, I was now ready to work on individual sections.

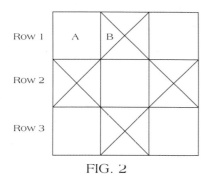

FIG. 2

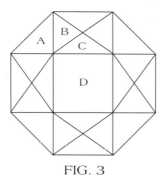

FIG. 3

When an Ohio Star block is drafted, it is usually done so in a square. But for my purposes I would be using all sorts of odd shapes. The Ohio Star is a Nine-Patch block. To draft the standard Ohio Star you begin with a square the size of your choice and divide it into nine equal sections. Then draw an X in the middle square in row 1, squares 1 and 3 in row 2, and the middle square in row 3. You would only need two templates (A and B) to piece this pattern (Fig. 2).

The moon was octagon-shaped, more like a square than many of the quilt's shapes, so I started there. To draft an Ohio Star in an octagon, I divided it in a similar fashion – it just appeared as if the corners were missing. I used the eight points of the octagon as if they were the eight points on the square. This gave a rounder, softer look to the moon element (Fig. 3).

GOTTA DANCE

In my full-size drawing I had already divided the earth with latitude and longitude lines, which created even more challenging shapes to draft within. Instead of two templates, each of these sections required 21 separate templates. Piecing the earth section required pre-planning.

I made a rough diagram to serve as a guide as I pieced. Then I cut the earth section away from the rest of my design and numbered the rows and each section (Fig. 4). The rows were then cut apart along latitude lines and each section was marked with a "T" at the top and a "B" at the bottom. By dividing the rows

along latitude lines, the stars would be skewed in a direction to give a more curved appearance to the earth element of the design.

The rows were then cut apart by sections. I tried to keep them in order; fortunately they were all numbered, just in case. Then I began drafting the star design into each section.

I had various sizes of plastic bags and a permanent black marker to mark and store each set of templates separately. I found it easier to do one row at a time starting with section 1-1. It helped to keep me oriented and able to visualize the results.

I used string, an 18-inch ruler, a mechanical pencil, and a white eraser. Because each section is odd-shaped, I laid it down in front of me with the side marked "T" at the top of the section, and the side marked "B" at the bottom. I used a string to measure the curved lines. Beginning with the top edge, I hold one end of the string at the top-left corner and lay the string along the top edge. When I arrived at the top-right corner, I pinched the string with my first finger and thumb. Holding the string, I moved it to the ruler and measured. I divided this measurement by three and marked my top edge with two

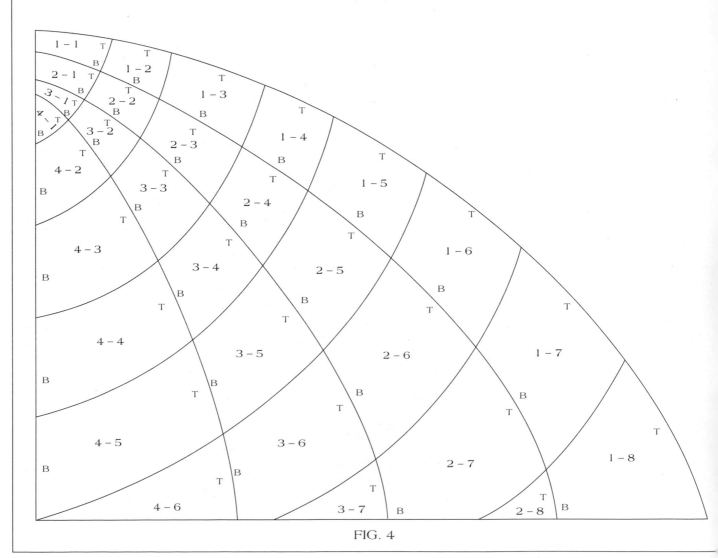

FIG. 4

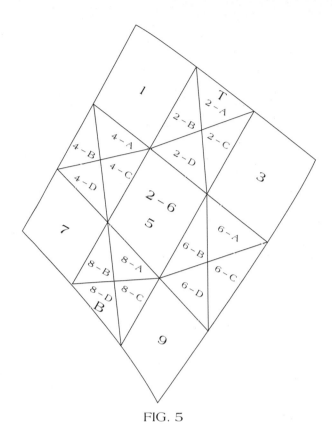

FIG. 5

dots or X's to divide it into three equal sections. This was repeated for the other three sides.

Then I took my ruler and connected the dots; top edge left dot to bottom edge left dot; top edge right dot to bottom edge right dot. Then I connected the left edge top dot to right edge top dot; left edge bottom dot to right edge bottom dot. This gave me very unequal sections.

I tried to imagine the section I was working with as a square with row 1, row 2, and row 3. I drew an X in the middle square of row 1. I completed the Ohio Star pattern by drawing an X in the same manner in row 2 squares 1 and 3 and the middle square in row 3. It is very important that all the sections are oriented in the same way ("T" the top and "B" the

bottom) so the stars are skewed in the same direction to achieve the curved appearance. I lettered and numbered each template of each section in the same manner (Fig. 5). Then I cut them apart, creating the pattern pieces needed for my design. I placed each section in a plastic bag and marked each bag with the section number.

Graduating the fabric values in the earth section also added to its rounded appearance. To accomplish this, I counted the number of sections, then chose my lightest and darkest values for the three elements in each section: tan background, green star points, and floral centers. The lightest value in the top left and the darkest in the bottom left of the earth. To choose the values

in between, I wanted to make sure they were evenly spaced (in terms of value) and moved smoothly from one to another – with one exception, where the dancer's spotlight ended.

The trail on the earth section (which is the reflection of the trail in space) was string-pieced and appliquéd on the finished earth section. The trail in the space section and the space section itself were pieced together using Caryl Bryer Fallert's string-piecing technique. This gave the trail its curving motion and gave the space its directional appearance.

Skewed Ohio Stars are repeated in the quilting in the space section, two with top stitching thread and others with metallic and the rayon.

USING A BLOCK TO FILL A DESIGN AREA
BY GENE P. H. IVES

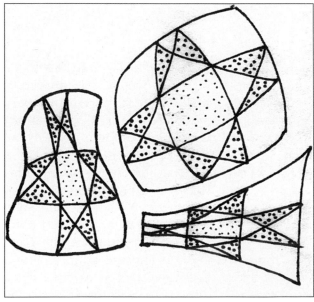

FIG. 1

■ Start with a basic shape contained within the overall shape of your quilt. It can be like the nearly yin-yang, tear drop shape I chose or a large wave-like shape, a lazy circle or a rounded corner box. Break each section into further smaller shapes – in jigsaw puzzle style. Using each one of these shapes, draw your block pattern, in this case the Ohio Star, inside it. The lines will not be straight and may not necessarily be parallel to each other (Fig. 1).

■ Then freehand draw your design on newsprint papers that have been taped together the size the completed quilt is to be. I tape mine to a wall. The freer your drawing the better. Don't try to be meticulous. Just let it flow. When you are happy with what you have drawn, go over the lines with a black magic marker (Fig 2). This will assist you in tracing your pattern. Next, it is very important that you number each piece.

■ Tape freezer paper together the same size as your original drawing and hang it over your drawing. Trace every piece making sure you also copy the number of each piece and mark the straight of the grain (Fig. 3, page 75). When sewing curves or angled pieces it is very important to keep pieces with the straight of the grain going north and south, or east and west. Another helpful thing is to make random marks that cross the pattern lines before cutting them apart, in order to facilitate matching pieces to one another. These marks on adjoining pieces function like the notches on dress patterns. Next cut out the pieces.

- Choose your colors and iron the freezer paper pattern pieces onto your selected fabric. When you cut the fabric out, be sure to add a ¼" seam allowance. Place the shiny side of freezer paper up on the master pattern for tracing if you want to iron the freezer paper pattern on the wrong side of the fabric, or place the dull side up if you like to work with the pattern on the right side of the fabric.

- I like to piece by hand. It has helped my gnarly arthritic hands immensely. (It beats doing the hand exercises the doctor recommends.) It is also easier for me to obtain accuracy by hand than by machine, but to each his own.

- Once you have tried this method, you will see that you can use this technique to experiment with other blocks. There's no limit to what you can do...and don't forget to share your knowledge with the next generation of quilters.

FIG. 2

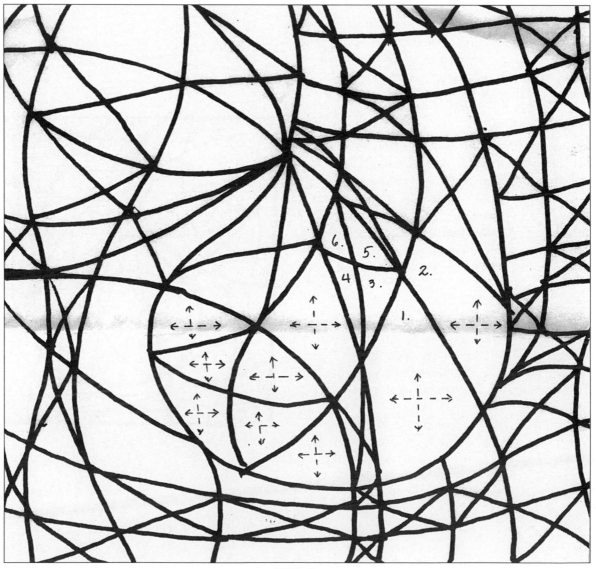

FIG. 3

WHY-O-WHY-OHIO

ADDING BORDERS TO QUILTS
BY MAGGIE POTTER

Detail of STAR FIELD, see full color quilt on page 16.

Many of the quilts I make have intricate borders. The many different patterned fabrics in my blocks generate a lot of movement. Borders are frequently needed to enclose this movement and prevent the eye from meandering off the quilt.

The border is added merely to enhance the overall design. I piece the center blocks first, often repeating no fabric combination more than once. When this is completed, I add one border at a time. If the quilt is elaborate in composition, I will use only one to two fabrics in the border. In STAR FIELD, the border colors were kept to a minimum. However, in the widest segment of the border, I used numerous colored fabrics so the border would not become too repetitious.

I used ½" strips of fabric in between the borders to ease the fabric into laying completely flat. I do not try to match the corners or make the borders connect perfectly. It's my belief a quilt should appear somewhat unplanned.

ADDITIONAL BORDERS BY MAGGIE POTTER

OHIO STAR QUILT, 70" x 82"

Detail of border of OHIO STAR QUILT

BROWN QUILT, 61" x 68"

Detail of border of BROWN QUILT

Photo by Jon Jensen

DESIGNING "OHIO LANDSCAPE"
BY GERTRUDE EMBREE

OHIO LANDSCAPE (top) and sketch for the quilt (bottom).

To plan my quilt, I developed a full working plan. I drew it on graph paper, letting each square of the grid equal ½", so it took four of the grid squares to equal one inch.

If you compare the graph paper drawing to the quilt, you will see I did not follow the drawing faithfully in all details. The placement of the main shapes is the same, but I improvised the centers of the "corner stars." There are a number of other ideas in the drawing that are not in the quilt...I changed my mind!

The pencil lines, especially visible on the lower right side, were my doodles for proposed quilting lines. Gayle Wallace, the quilter, used a different design.

In a drawing like this the color placement indicated is only approximate. This design becomes a general guide rather than a precise plan that must be followed in every detail.

Patterns from the Quilts

MAKING OHIO STAR
CHICKENFISH
BY NANCY S. BROWN

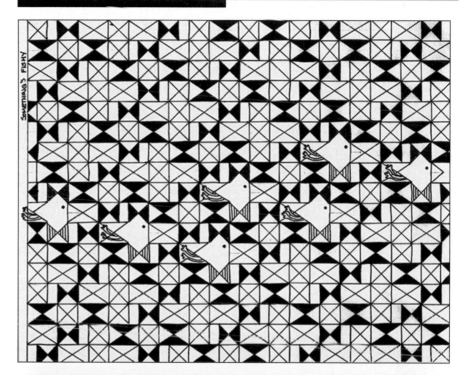

When I discovered that my elongated Ohio Star blocks could be turned into fish and Chickenfish, I had great fun coloring in the overall design I'd drawn. Patterns follow in case you'd like to experiment with these creatures yourselves.

Pattern pieces are on page 82 and appliqué shapes can be traced from the full-size block drawing on page 83.

Black and white layout diagram (top) and full-color diagram (above) for SOMETHING'S FISHY

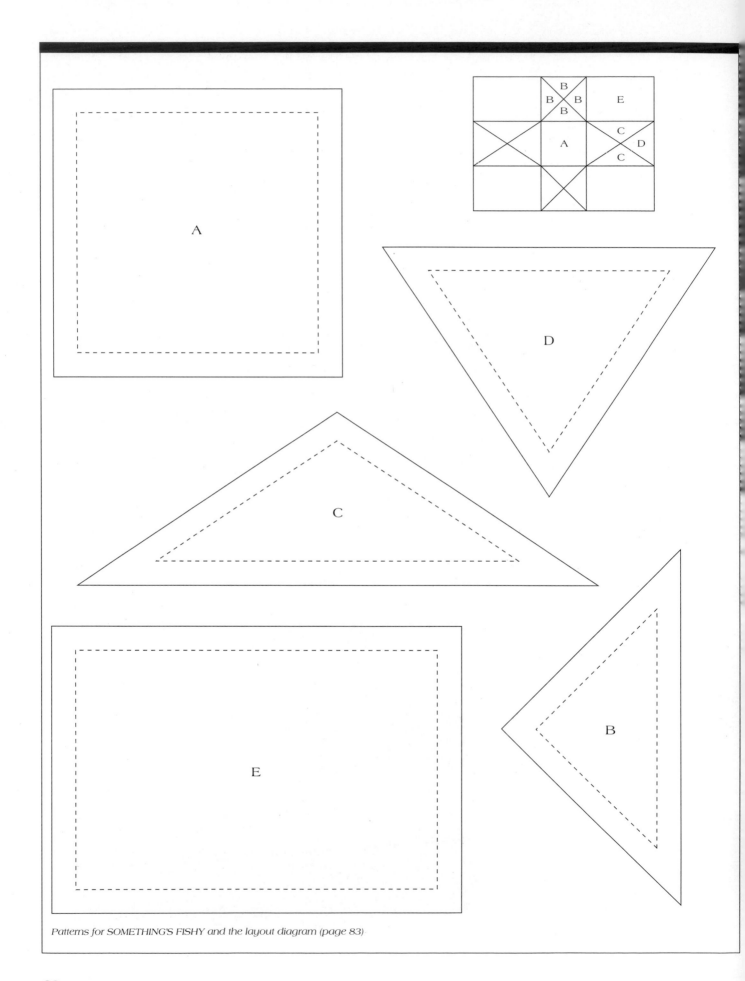

Patterns for SOMETHING'S FISHY and the layout diagram (page 83)

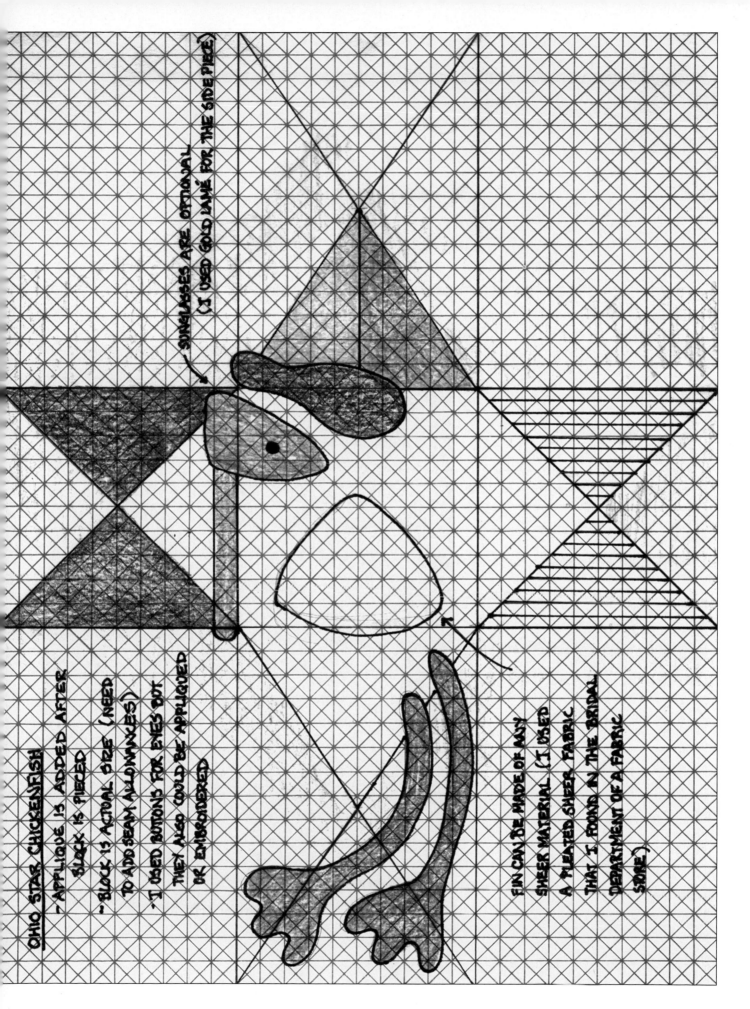

SUNGLASSES ARE OPTIONAL
(I USED GOLD LAMÉ FOR THE SIDE PIECE)

OHIO STAR CHICKEN/FISH

- APPLIQUÉ IS ADDED AFTER
  BLOCK IS PIECED

- BLOCK IS ACTUAL SIZE (NEED
  TO ADD SEAM ALLOWANCES)

- I USED BUTTONS FOR EYES BUT
  THEY ALSO COULD BE APPLIQUÉD
  OR EMBROIDERED

FIN CAN BE MADE OF MANY
SHEER MATERIAL (I USED
A PLEATED SHEER FABRIC
THAT I FOUND IN THE BRIDAL
DEPARTMENT OF A FABRIC
STORE)

PATTERNS FOR "AN OLD MASK"
BY JUDY BECKER

My mask series of quilts is basically autobiographical. Women wear many masks in life, often as a response to the multiple roles we assume in a complex culture. These masks are protective camouflage. In SELF PORTRAITS, shown right, the masks were clearly influenced by my admiration for Oceanic, African, and Cubist art. This quilt is a quixotic look at some of my fantasy disguises.

AN OLD MASK, my Ohio Star quilt, is part of my mask series. A pattern for the mask used in my Ohio Star quilt appears on page 85, and a full-size pattern for the linear design in the background appears on page 87.

SELF PORTRAITS, 53" x 75", Judy Becker

PATTERN FOR: "AN OLD MASK"

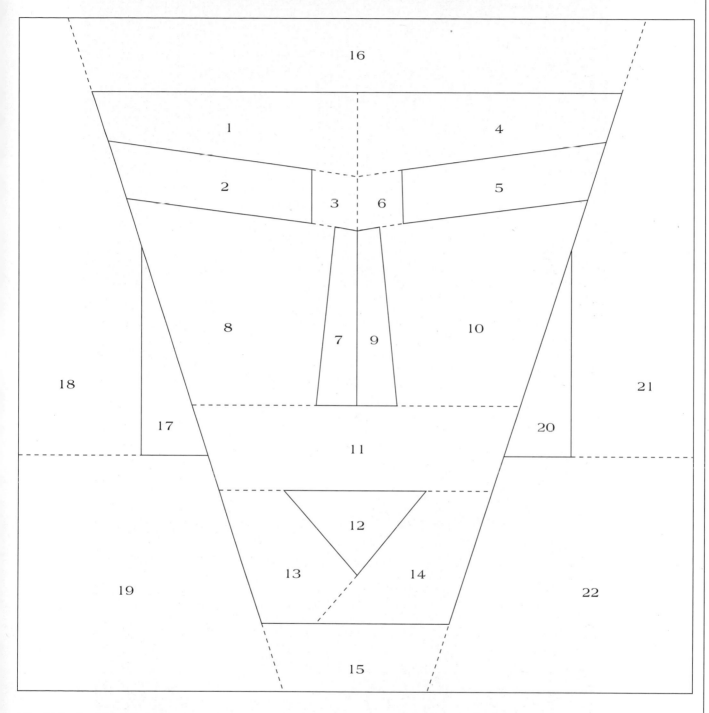

Final block size: 14"
½" = 1"; Drawing scale

A. Sew 1, 2, 3 together & 4, 5, 6

B. Sew 7 & 8, then 9 & 10

C. Sew 1, 2, 3 & 7, 8. Then 4, 5, 6 & 9, 10

D. Sew 1, 2, 3, 7, 8 & 4, 5, 6, 9, 10

E. Sew 12 & 13, then 14

F. Sew assembled strips for face in order adding 15 & 16

G. Sew 17, 18 & add 19
   Sew 20, 21 & add 22

H. Sew both side triangles to face

TOP: *ANONYMOUS WAS A WOMAN, 62" x 47", Judy Becker*
ABOVE: *ONLY IN NEW YORK, 59" x 46", Judy Becker*

PATTERN FOR BACKGROUND: "AN OLD MASK"

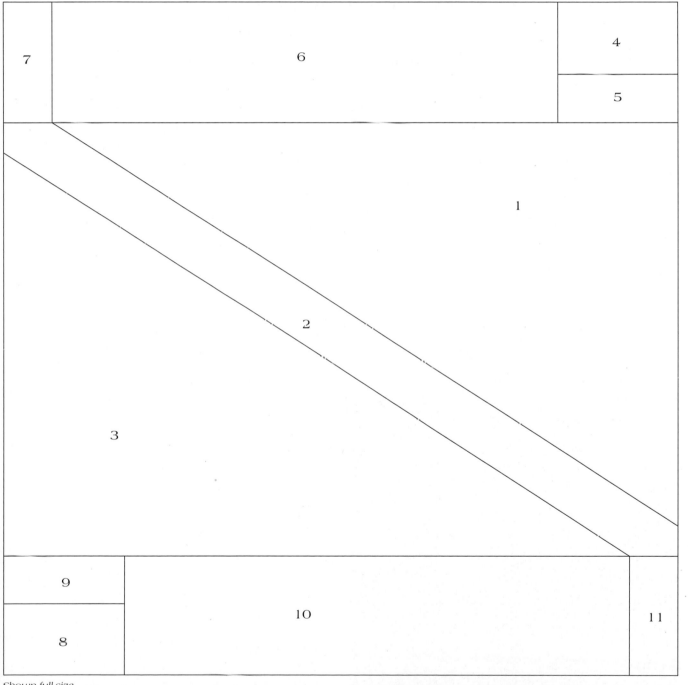

Shown full-size

USING APPLIQUÉD STRIPS TO CREATE OHIO STAR BLOCKS
BY CORINNE APPLETON

ALL CATS GO TO HEAVEN began with the idea of distorting the basic Ohio Star block. Working with the Electric Quilt® computer program, I decided to keep the blocks themselves square, but to distort the star within the boundaries of the block. When the idea of emphasizing the blocks' lines by using appliquéd strips made its way into my consciousness, the concept of each block being slightly different than the others seemed appropriate.

There are many ways you could modify my quilt. Think of the defining strips as frames. The quilt block centers could feature family and friends' portraits; even a small Ohio Star block could be drafted and fit within the confines of the larger star (Fig. 1).

The finished size of the blocks in ALL CATS GO TO HEAVEN is 14½", but the directions given use a 15½" square to simplify the math.

Step 1

Cut one 15½" square from your background fabric. Starch the block to stabilize it. If you are using one or two background fabrics for the entire quilt, starch the fabrics as yardage and then cut your blocks from the fabrics.

The most important rule when spray starching your fabric is to give the starch plenty of time to be absorbed into the fibers before ironing. I often spray a group of fabrics, roll them up, then clean and oil my sewing machine before ironing.

If you are using yardage you can then iron as usual. If you have pre-cut your blocks it is important

ALL CATS GO TO HEAVEN

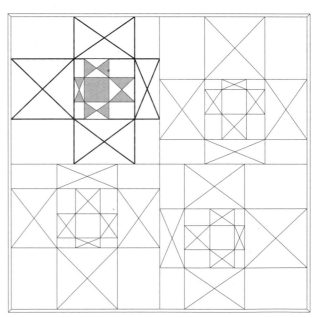

FIG. 1

that you press your blocks. Running the iron back and forth will leave you moaning over a pile of blocks that once were square.

Step 2

To design your distorted block, choose the size and position you will use for the center of your Ohio Star. You have two options for the block center and will probably want to vary them both in your quilt.

First, your center can be cut to the traditional ⅑ of the surface area of the block. With a finished size of 15" x 15", this means a 5" x 5" square.

Alternatively, you can cut a square or rectangle in any measurement that is close to the traditional center square size, but

slightly "off." Even very small changes in the size are effective: try 4½" x 5½", or 5" x 6".

The effectiveness of your block center depends as much upon its placement on the background as it does upon its altered size. Place your block center in the approximate middle of your background square. If your center is a rectangle or a square smaller than five inches you may choose to make this the permanent position for the center.

NOTE: If you are using a 5" square it is essential to the block design that you move your center so that it is not in the middle of the block (Fig. 2). Otherwise, you will end up with a traditional Ohio Star block rather than the distorted version we are making.

All of the blocks used in ALL

CATS GO TO HEAVEN consist of centers that were first placed roughly in the middle of the background and then moved a small distance.

Step 3

Cut a 15½" x 2¼" piece of paper-backed fusible web. Fuse it to the back of the fabric you have chosen to define your star, preferably on the lengthwise grain. From this piece cut four ½" wide strips. It is easier to cut through both the paper-backed fusible web and the fabric at once; take advantage of your extra quarter inch of width and begin your first cut slightly to the inside of it and you will achieve a straighter edge.

Peel the paper backing from your four 15½" x ½" strips.

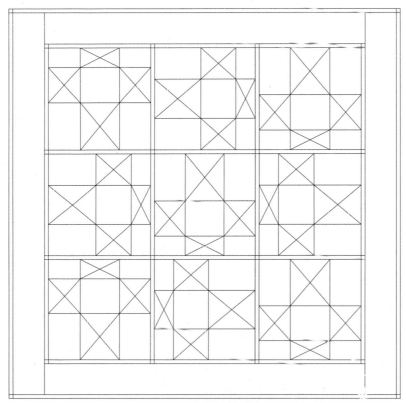

Distorted Ohio Star blocks with all centers the same size

FIG. 2

Step 4

Using a ruler to ensure you are an even distance from the edge of your quilt block, place a ½" strip from Step 3 on one of the four edges of your center square or rectangle. The placement of this strip should overlap the center's edge by ¼" so that the fusible web covers both the center and the background fabric equally along the length of the center's edge (Fig. 3).

With your iron set to the appropriate temperature, fuse the strip to the block as follows: use the iron tip to fuse the area between the outside edge of the block and the point where the strip meets the center square or rectangle. Leave approximately 1" *unfused* at the outside edge and at the area where the strip and center meet. Next, fuse the strip over the center square or rectangle, being careful to avoid that 1" area on both sides of the center. Finally repeat the fusing directions on the portion of your ½" strip that extends to the other side of the block.

These steps are repeated three times to form an irregular Nine-Patch, as shown in Fig. 4.

HINT: If at any point in the construction of your block you discover you have accidentally fused a portion of a defining strip you didn't want fused, don't worry. The simple remedy is to apply the iron to that area until the glue softens and the fabric can be lifted gently, using a pin or seam ripper to release the edge. Be careful not to distort the strip by tugging or pulling; with enough time and heat the adhesive will release.

One other word of caution: do not let your freshly unglued

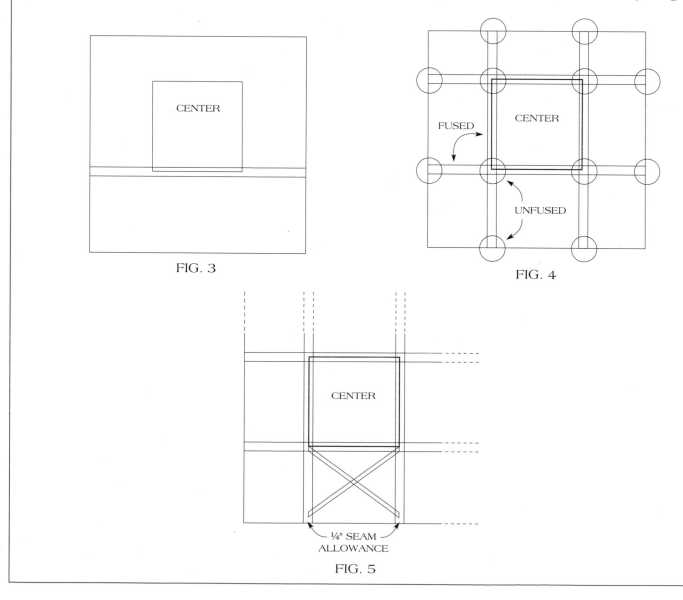

FIG. 3

FIG. 4

FIG. 5

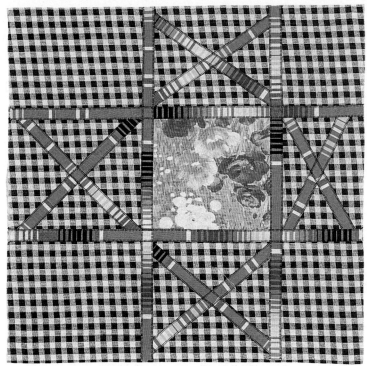

This block was intended to be one of the nine in ALL CATS GO TO HEAVEN but instead became an orphan after teaching me a lesson. The contrast between the crooked checks and the rigidly straight defining strips made the quilt top scream "TILT." If you use checks or plaids with this block pattern, be sure that they are printed or woven straight. Also, make sure that your defining strips are laid exactly parallel to the straight lines of the fabric's pattern.

appliqué piece touch itself.

Prepare another 2¼" wide piece of your strip fabric with fusible web. Try to get the maximum length possible from your yardage. Cut the piece into ½" wide strips.

The next step in making your star is to fill in the X that creates the points. This is not a step that requires precision measuring and there is no formula as this is where the diversity in your blocks shows up. It helps to begin by cutting one end of a ½" strip at an angle of about 45 degrees. Using a pin, wiggle that cut end under the intersection of one of the corners of your center. With a pin or a finger holding that end in place but allowing it to pivot, follow an imaginary diagonal line to create a star point. The star tip should be embellished with a button or other object so that the tip appears defined and not blunted. The second option is to lay the diagonal strip on top of the straight strip and carefully cut the diagonal strip on an angle to match the edge of the straight strip. This option creates a sharper point that requires no embellishment.

Choose the style of point you want and prepare your fabric strip, always remembering this golden rule; *the diagonal strips always end ¼" from the block edge* to

allow for a seam allowance (Fig. 5). If you think you will have any difficulty remembering this rule, mark your block ¼" in on every straight ½" strip after they are in place. Just remember to use a marking method that will not become permanent with the application of a hot iron.

Once your diagonal strips are in place the iron is laid over both the previously unfused straight strip's outside edge and the length of the diagonal to where it just touches the center. Only when all of the strips have been fused as described should the iron be applied to the center intersections (where it fuses two diagonal ends beneath two intersecting straight strips at the same time).

Step 5

Your block is now ready for appliqué. Put a new size 70 heavy duty needle in your cleaned and oiled machine and thread it with your choice of contrasting or matching thread.

With a piece of stabilizer beneath your block (commercial stabilizer is typing-weight paper), the next step is the stitching.

The appliqué can be done with any number of decorative stitches, or a simple zigzag. ALL CATS GO TO HEAVEN uses a black blanket stitch to contrast with the multicolored stripe of its defining strips; BEYOND ECCENTRIC AND PUSHING CRAZY was appliquéd with a very narrow and short zigzag done in black so as to blend into the defining strips and not to distract from the planned chaos of the stars.

The most important technical contribution you can make to the success of your quilt block is to ensure that the line of appliqué is as straight as the edge of the ½" strips that outline your star.

Stitch the long straight strips first, making sure to backstitch at the end of each strip. The diagonal strips can be backstitched at their ends by machine if your thread and fabric are both dark and a perfect match. In most cases, you will find the appearance far preferable if you tug the upper thread to the reverse side, tie a square knot, and thread the ends through a row of stitches.

Once all the stitching is complete, turn the block over and remove your stabilizer. Carefully cut away the background fabric from beneath the center square or rectangle. Give your block a pressing, stick it up on your design wall, admire it, and then get busy making another one!

BEYOND ECCENTRIC AND PUSHING CRAZY, 47" x 47", 1996

PATTERNS FOR "RED SKY AT NIGHT"
BY DEANNA D. DISON

This diamond block which contains a modified Ohio Star block was developed using computer software, as was the overall quilt design. A computer printout is shown left.

On the following pages are full-size patterns for making the block, along with a grid of blocks for planning your own quilt.

ABOVE: *Full-color computer printout of the quilt design*
RIGHT: *Layout for Ohio Star block*

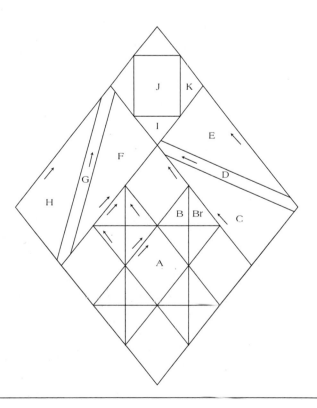

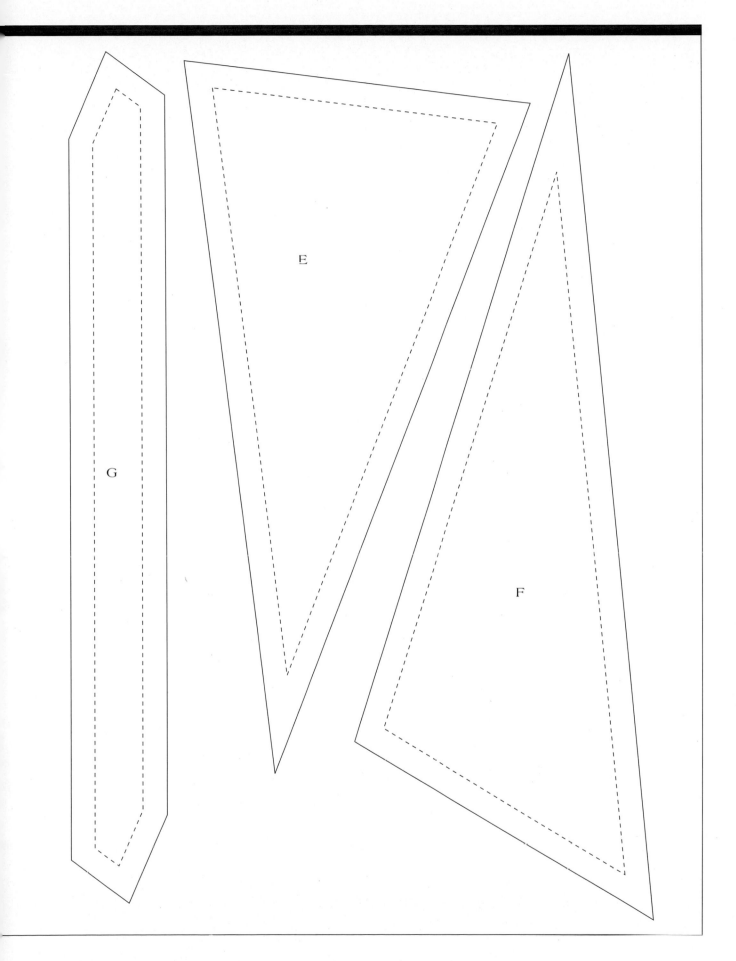

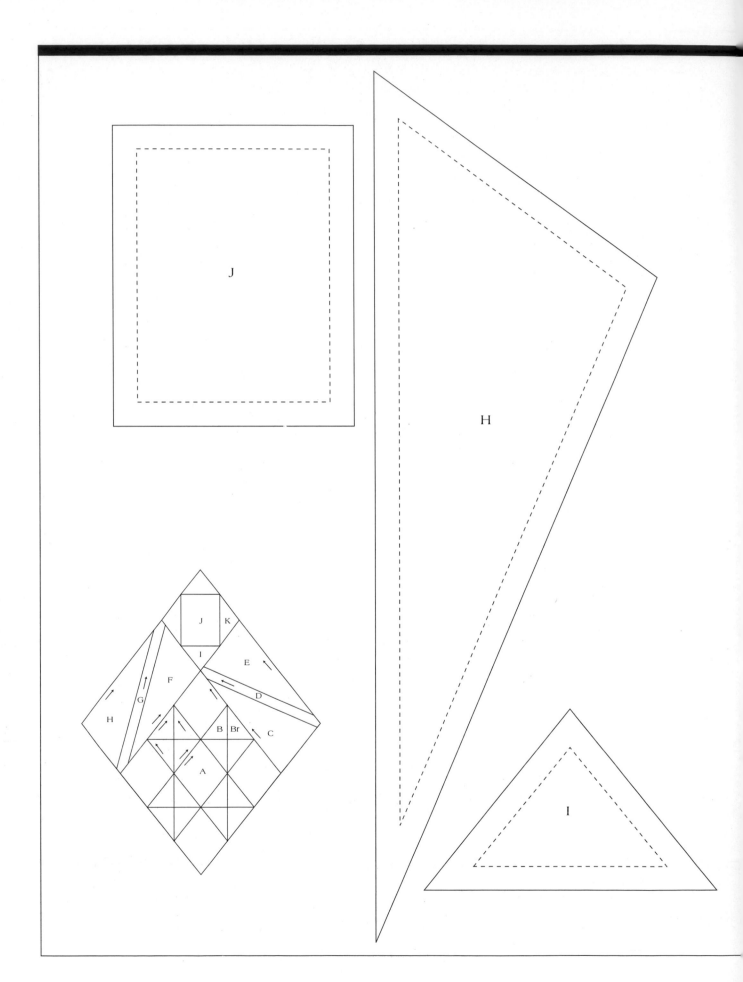

OVERALL DESIGN: "RED SKY AT NIGHT"

Full quilt with 4" borders: 57 x 70½"

MAKING "JOURNEY"
BY SUSAN STEIN

Quilt size: 60" x 72"

Materials:

- One 8-step half-yard bundle of dyed fabric (rust to turquoise)
- One 6-step fat-quarter bundle of dyed fabric (rust)
- 1¾ yards print fabric for background
- 1¼ yards solid color fabric for inner border and binding
- 3½ yards fabric for backing

Instructions:

1. Cut three 5¼" squares of the first two and last two values of rust fabric and four 5¼" squares of values 3 and 4 of the rust fabric. Cut with an X through each square, cutting diagonally, corner to corner, in both directions (Fig. 1).

2. Cut eighty 4½" squares of print. Cut twenty 5¼" squares of print and slice into triangles as above.

3. From the large bundle of dyed fabric, cut:

    Step 1 – one 4½" square and two 5¼" squares, cut with an X

    Step 2 – two 4½" squares and four 5¼" squares, cut with an X

    Step 3 – three 4½" squares and six 5¼" squares, cut with an X

    Step 4 – four 4½" squares and eight 5¼" squares, cut with an X

    Step 5 – four 4½" squares and eight 5¼" squares, cut with an X

    Step 6 – three 4½" squares and six 5¼" squares, cut with an X

    Step 7 – two 4½" squares and four 5¼" squares, cut with an X

    Step 8 – one 4½" square and two 5¼" squares, cut with an X

4. Piece 20 Ohio Star blocks, using the 4½" squares and triangles cut from 5¼" squares.

Use the lightest rust fabric for the three blocks in the upper left corner and the darkest rust fabric for three blocks in lower right corner. The four middle values of rust are used diagonally, one to a row. The turquoise to rust fabrics are used one color per diagonal row, beginning with the turquoise in the upper left and ending with the rust in the lower right. See page 99.

5. Cut the inner border strips 2½" wide. To make an outer border like mine, you will need 62 additional squares cut 4½".

6. My petroglyphs (see page 100) are cut with no seam allowances and top stitched down with raw edges exposed.

7. Add the borders and petroglyphs or shapes of your own choice.

8. The binding is cut 2½" wide.

9. Quilt and add binding.

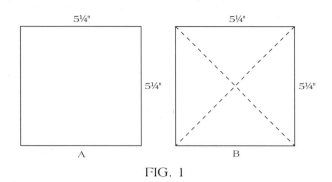

FIG. 1

COLOR PLACEMENT GUIDE – QUILT CENTER IN "JOURNEY"

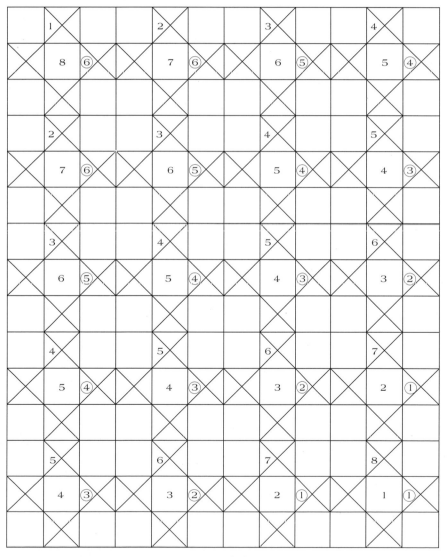

①–⑥: rust, ⑥ being lightest

1 – 8 : turquoise – rust, 1 being turquoise and 8 being rust

PETROGLYPHS FOR "JOURNEY"
SHOWN AT 50%

ROTARY CUTTING
"WITHOUT ORANGE, THERE IS NO BLUE"
BY SUE SPIGEL

ORGANIZING THE FABRICS

This multi-fabric quilt was made with seven different color (hue) families, each of which was graded from dark to light.

Background fabric:

- Golds (light cream through dark brown)

Star Fabrics (points, inner and outer squares):

- Dark to light navy
- Blue-purple, dark to light
- Purple, dark to light
- Red, dark to light
- Red-orange, dark to light
- Orange, dark to light

THE OHIO STAR BLOCK

The block in this quilt is a finished size of 6". There are two main pattern pieces in the block, a square for the center and four corners, and a quarter square triangle, with its long side on the straight of grain (Fig. 1).

As this quilt was rotary cut, all the squares were cut from strips 2½" wide and all the triangles were cut from strips 1⅝" wide. These measurements include ¼" seam allowance.

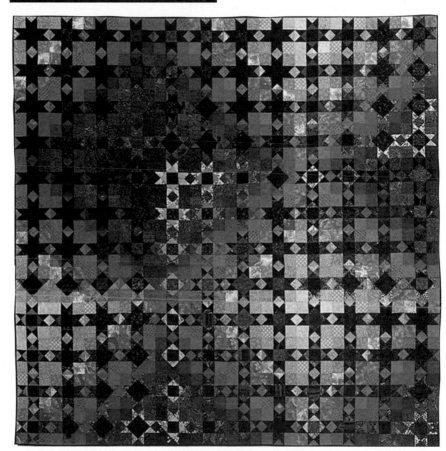

WITHOUT ORANGE, THERE IS NO BLUE

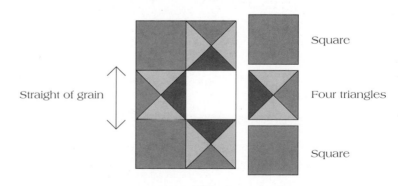

Straight of grain

Square

Four triangles

Square

FIG. 1

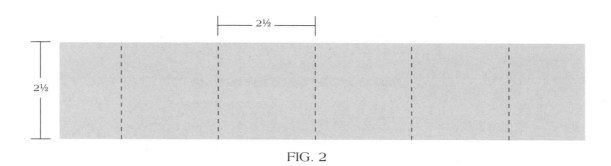

FIG. 2

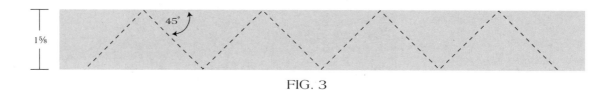

FIG. 3

CUTTING THE FABRIC

Two strips were cut from each of the fabrics, one 2½" wide and the other 1⅝" wide, and as long as the entire width of the fabric. Squares were cut from the 2½" strip (Fig. 2).

Triangles were cut from the 1⅝" strip using the 45 degree angle on the ruler (Fig. 3).

FABRIC PLACEMENT

The patchwork was done in 4 x 4 units of Ohio Stars, shading each of the block components (background, star points, outer squares on point, and inner squares) in a different direction. Fig. 4 is a sample of how a unit might be shaded, but as I was actually cutting each of my units in fabric, I changed the shading direction and areas to suit my whim, just to see what I would get.

First, the background pieces were placed on a felt board shading diagonally dark to light from one corner to the opposite corner, as shown in Fig. 4.

Then the star points, navys, were added, shading dark at the top to light at the bottom (Fig. 5).

Next, the outer squares (on point, surrounding the center inner square) were shaded diagonally from light to dark purple-blue, in the opposite direction to the background shading (Fig. 6).

Finally, the inner squares were shaded dark purple at the bottom to light purple at the top (Fig. 7).

CONSTRUCTION

In all nine 4 x 4 units were designed in fabric and then pieced, to create the final quilt.

COMPUTER PRINTOUTS: DEVELOPING THE 4 X 4 UNIT DESIGN

FIG. 4

FIG. 5

FIG. 6

FIG. 7

COMPUTER PRINTOUTS FOR THE NINE 4 X 4 UNITS

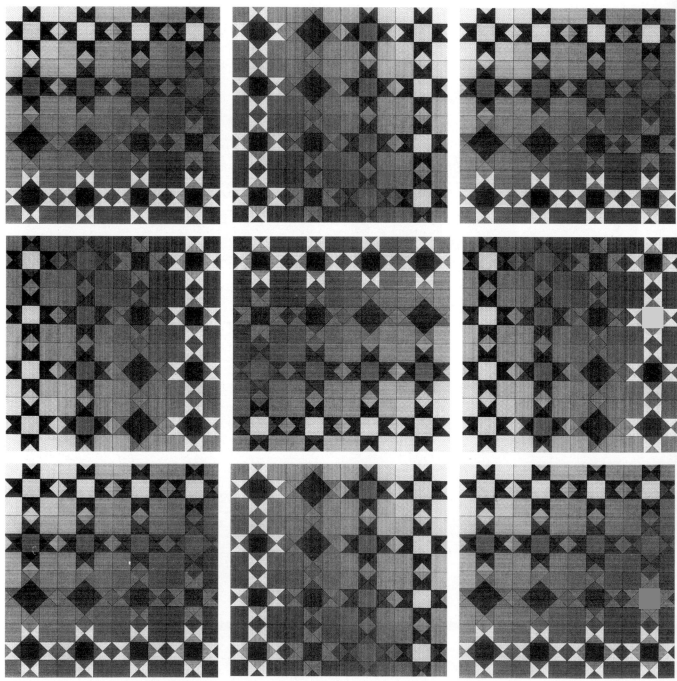

Computer printouts arranged to suggest over all final layout of WITHOUT ORANGE, THERE IS NO BLUE.

MAKING "RIVERS OF DESTINY"
BY GERI KINNEAR

RIVERS OF DESTINY

QUILT SIZE: 54" x 54"

BLOCK SIZE: 10" square

MATERIALS

- Light and dark blue fabric
- 9 bright prints in different colors
- Double faced fusing material
- Beads – assorted sizes and shapes
- Decorative threads
- Batting
- Fabric for border, binding, and backing

CUTTING

Cut 32 light blue 3" squares, 48 dark blue 3" squares

Cut 20 light blue 5½" squares, 20 dark blue 5½" squares

Cut 5 light blue 10½" squares, 5 dark blue 10½" squares

RIVERS OF DESTINY

ASSEMBLY

Following the manufacturer's directions, bond fusible web to the bright colored print fabrics. I cut the squares and triangles for the stars without using templates, because I wanted the stars to appear joyful and free floating on the blue background. However, feel free to use the templates on page 107 for the stars.

Check the photograph of RIVERS OF DESTINY (page 105) for the correct number of stars needed for each diagonal line of stars. Remove the backing papers and position the star shapes on the appropriate square. Be sure to position all star points ¼" from the cut edge so they don't fall in the seam allowance.

I usually do my bonding on the ironing board, and bond several stars at a time. However, it was easier to bond the 10½" stars on a sturdy table, with several thicknesses of towels on it.

Because the 3" blocks were so tiny, I decided not to satin stitch around each piece of the stars. I machine straight stitched around the edge of each piece, and pulled the threads to the back, tying them twice. This took a long time, but it produced a secure, flat surface, and prevents future problems of unraveling.

Assemble the sixteen 3" blocks together, forming five 10½" squares, making sure that the four tiny stars run on the diagonal, from top right to bottom left.

Assemble the four 5½" blocks together, forming ten 10½" squares, again checking for the diagonal.

Join the finished squares into rows, and assemble the rows.

Add a 2½" border.

QUILTING

I machine quilted close to the edges of each star. This helps the stars stand out. The quilt is also quilted in wavy lines to emphasize the feeling of water. I also couched Madeira #8 Glamour thread, leaving the edges of the threads loose.

RIVERS OF DESTINY is quite striking on its own, but when I found bags of assorted sizes and shapes of white beads, I bought them on the spot! I knew they would add an intensity of feeling to my work. Be sure to use beading thread and large knots when placing beads on a quilt.

Detail of RIVERS OF DESTINY

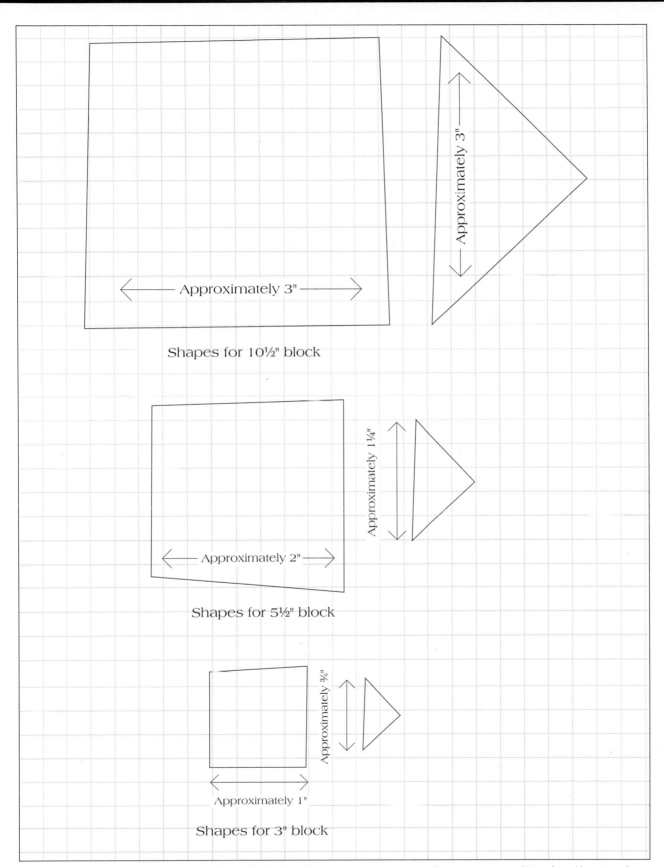

Approximately 3"

Approximately 3"

Shapes for 10½" block

Approximately 1¼"

Approximately 2"

Shapes for 5½" block

Approximately ¾"

Approximately 1"

Shapes for 3" block

Note – Shapes are not square in order to produce a free floating effect. Readers are encouraged to cut squares and triangles without templates.

The Quiltmakers

The Quilts

The Museum

MUSEUM OF THE AMERICAN QUILTER'S SOCIETY
215 Jefferson Street, Paducah, Kentucky

A dream long held by American Quilter's Society founders Bill and Meredith Schroeder and by quilters worldwide was realized on April 25, 1991, when the Museum of the American Quilter's Society (MAQS, pronounced "Max") opened its doors in Paducah, Kentucky. As is stated in brass lettering over the building's entrance, this non-profit institution is dedicated to "honoring today's quilter," by stimulating and supporting the study, appreciation, and development of quiltmaking throughout the world.

The 30,000 square foot facility includes a center exhibition gallery featuring a selection of the 160 quilts by contemporary quilt-makers comprising the Schroeder/MAQS Collection, and two additional galleries displaying exhibits of antique and contemporary quilts. Lectures, workshops, and other related activities are also held on site, in spacious modern classrooms. A gift and book shop makes available a wide selection of fine crafts and quilt books. The museum is open year-round, Tuesdays through Saturdays, and is wheelchair accessible.

For more information, write: MAQS, P.O. Box 1540, Paducah, KY 42002-1540, or phone: 502-442-8856.

Other MAQS Publications

Amish Kinder Komforts: The Sara Miller Collection
Bettina Havig
#4696: AQS, 1996, 88 pages, 8½" x 11", softbound, $14.95.

Anna Williams: Her Quilts and Their Influence
Katherine Watts
#4624: AQS, 1995, 40 pages, 8½" x 11", softbound, $12.95.

Antique Quilts from the Miriam Tuska Collection
#4625: AQS, 1995, 40 pages, 6" x 9", softbound, $12.95.

Caryl Bryer Fallert: A Spectrum of Quilts 1983–1995
Caryl Bryer Fallert
#4697: AQS, 1996, 112 pages, 8¼" x 10¾", softbound, $24.95.

Contemporary Quilts from The James Collection
Ardis James
#4525: AQS, 1995, 40 pages, 6" x 9", softbound, $12.95.

Double Wedding Ring Quilts: New Quilts from an Old Favorite
Edited by Victoria Faoro
#3870: AQS, 1994, 112 pages, 8½" x 11", softbound, $14.95.

Gatherings: America's Quilt Heritage
Kathlyn F. Sullivan
#4526: AQS, 1995, 224 pages, 10" x 8½", softbound, $34.95.

Log Cabin Quilts: New Quilts from an Old Favorite
Edited by Victoria Faoro
#4523, AQS, 1995, 112 pages, 8½" x 11", softbound, $14.95.

The Log Cabin Returns to Kentucky: Quilts from the Pilgrim/Roy Collection
Paul D. Pilgrim and Gerald E. Roy
#3329: AQS, 1992, 36 pages, 9" x 7", softbound, $12.95.

Nancy Crow: Quilts and Influences
Nancy Crow
#1981: AQS, 1990, 256 pages, 9" x 12", hardcover, $29.95.

Nancy Crow: Work in Transition
Nancy Crow
#3331: AQS, 1992, 32 pages, 9" x 10", softbound, $12.95.

New Jersey Quilts – 1777 to 1950: Contributions to an American Tradition
The Heritage Quilt Project of New Jersey
#3332: AQS, 1992, 256 pages, 8½" x 11", softbound, $29.95.

Quilts: Old and New, A Similar View
Paul D. Pilgrim and Gerald E. Roy
#3715: AQS, 1993, 40 pages, 8¾" x 8", softbound, $12.95.

Quilts: The Permanent Collection – MAQS
#2257: AQS, 1991, 100 pages, 10" x 6½", softbound, $9.95.

Quilts: The Permanent Collection, Volume II – MAQS
#3793: AQS, 1994, 80 pages, 10" x 6½", softbound, $9.95.

Victorian Quilts, 1875–1900: They Aren't All Crazy
Paul D. Pilgrim and Gerald E. Roy
#3932: AQS, 1994, 64 pages, 6" x 9", softbound, $14.95.

These books can be found in the MAQS book shop and in local bookstores and quilt shops. If you are unable to locate a title in your area, you can order by mail from the publisher:

American Quilter's Society
P.O. Box 3290, Paducah, KY 42002-3290

Please add $2 for the first book and $.40 for each additional one to cover postage and handling.
International orders please add $2.50 for the first book and $1 for each additional one.

To order by VISA or MASTERCARD call: 1-800-626-5420 or fax: 1-502-898-8890.

AQS BOOKS ON QUILTS

This is only a partial listing of the books on quilts that are available from the American Quilter's Society. AQS books are known the world over for their timely topics, clear writing, beautiful color photographs, and accurate illustrations and patterns. Most of the following books are available from your local bookseller, quilt shop, or public library. If you are unable to locate certain titles in your area, you may order by mail from the AMERICAN QUILTER'S SOCIETY, P.O. Box 3290, Paducah, KY 42002-3290. Customers with Visa or MasterCard may phone in orders from 7:00–4:00 CST, Monday–Friday, Toll Free 1-800-626-5420. Add $2.00 for postage for the first book ordered and $0.40 for each additional book. Include item number, title, and price when ordering. Allow 14 to 21 days for delivery.

112